Fulfilled & Limitless

A Blueprint For Leading Powerfully Without Losing Yourself

by

CHRISTI COSSETTE

Copyright © 2025 by Christi Cossette and Cossette Transformation Coaching. All rights reserved. No part of this book or its associated ancillary materials may be reproduced or transmitted in any form or by any means, electronic or mechanical, including photocopying, recording, or by any informational storage or retrieval system, without permission from the author or publisher.

Published by Jumpstart Publishing, PO Box 6, Roseville, CA 95661. (916) 872-4000 www.JumpstartPublishing.net

DISCLAIMER AND/OR LEGAL NOTICES

This book is intended for informational and inspirational purposes only. It does not constitute professional advice, diagnosis, or treatment in mental health, medical care, financial services, or legal counsel. Readers are encouraged to seek guidance from qualified professionals as needed.

Every individual's journey toward fulfillment is unique. While this book offers strategies, insights, and encouragement, outcomes may vary based on personal circumstances, individual effort, and external factors beyond the author's control.

The stories and experiences shared in this book are personal to the author and are intended to illustrate key principles. They do not intend to suggest that all readers experience the same results. Any examples, case studies, or references are provided for illustrative purposes only. They should not be interpreted as typical results or guarantees of success.

This book is written from a Christian faith perspective. Readers of all backgrounds are welcome, and references to faith are intended to encourage reflection and empowerment, regardless of personal belief systems.

ISBN: 979-8-9995282-1-6

Printed in the United States.

Written By Ashley Hawks

There's a quiet courage in the moment a woman finally asks herself, *"Is this really it?"* Not because she's ungrateful—but because something inside her knows she was made for more.

When my friend Christi asked me to write this foreword, I felt incredibly honored—not just because of the beautiful message in these pages, but because I've lived through the tension this book speaks to. I went back to work way too soon after having my babies—pumping in parking lots, missing first steps, and running on fumes, convinced it was just the cost of success. Then my health collapsed. An autoimmune flare left me barely able to get out of bed, feeling like a stranger in my own body. And through it all, my marriage was hanging on by a thread. I was burning out mentally, physically, emotionally—and spiritually. I know what it feels like to be "successful" on paper and completely disconnected from myself in real life.

That's why this book matters so much. *Fulfilled & Limitless* offers more than inspiration—it offers **permission.** Permission to slow down, to realign, to question the scripts we've been handed about success, motherhood, leadership, and worth. It reminds you that you're not selfish for wanting more joy, more energy, more peace— and that wanting more doesn't mean doing more. It means becoming more of who you already are.

I now run a peer group organization for CEOs and business leaders who want success in all areas of life, and I've seen firsthand what happens when people step into environments that are honest, intentional, and supportive. They come back to life. They find their fire again! That's what this book does. It sparks something. It doesn't hand you answers—it helps you ask the *right* questions. The kind that awakens your truth and unlocks your next chapter.

If you've ever wondered if there's more to life than your current version of "success," this book is for you. Read it slowly. Let it speak to you. Because sometimes, the breakthrough we need doesn't come from pushing harder—but from finally pausing long enough to listen.

Ashley Hawks, Founder

SOAR Leadership Groups

Acknowledgements

First and foremost, I want to thank my husband, Andy—my greatest supporter, my steady encouragement, and my true partner in life. Your unwavering belief in me, even in the seasons when the path was unclear, has given me the strength to keep moving forward. Thank you for standing beside me, lifting me up, and sharing this journey with me. I am endlessly grateful to do life with you.

To my three amazing boys—Brady, Mason, and Preston—you are my greatest joy and constant inspiration. I hope you always know how deeply you are loved and how limitless your futures are.

To my extended family and dear friends—thank you for your love, prayers, and encouragement through every season of growth. Your presence in my life has been a gift beyond measure.

To my clients and the incredible women I've had the honor of coaching—your courage, authenticity, and pursuit of a fulfilled life inspire the very heartbeat of this work. Thank you for trusting me to walk alongside you.

And above all, I thank my Lord and Savior, Jesus Christ. Every word written, every lesson learned, and every ounce of courage and resilience to complete this journey has come from You. May this work bring You glory and encourage others to walk fully in the calling You have placed on their lives.

Table Of Contents

Introduction: The Path To A Fulfilled & Limitless Life..................1

Part 1: The Fulfilled Life Formula.................................. 8
    Chapter 1: The Fulfilled Life Formula 9
    Chapter 2: Identity.. 23
    Chapter 3: Energy... 46
    Chapter 4: Purpose 66
        Faith.. 68
        Love... 78
        Meaningful Work 109
    Chapter 5: Growth 121
    Chapter 6: Living For Something Bigger 145

Part 2: Implementation.. 155
    Chapter 7: Building The Life Of Your Dreams 156
    Chapter 8: Building Habits & Routines To Support Your Roadmap.. 176
    Chapter 9: Overcoming "Failure" And Setbacks 194
    Chapter 10: Overcoming Roadblocks 200
    Chapter 11: Stop Settling And Ask For What You Need 252
    Chapter 12: Celebrate Your Wins & Savor The Joys In Life.... 258
    Chapter 13: Keeping The Momentum....................... 271
    Conclusion: A Love Letter To You............................. 282
    About The Author.. 286
    Bibliography... 288
    Additional Resources 290

Introduction

The Path To A Fulfilled & Limitless Life

There comes a moment in every woman's life when she looks around and wonders, *Is this really it?* On the outside, everything may seem perfect. A successful career, a beautiful family, a life that others admire. And yet, something inside whispers that there's more—that she was made for more. Not just more success and achievement, but more depth, joy, and fulfillment.

For years, I chased the version of success I was told would bring happiness. I worked hard, climbed the corporate ladder, built a business, and did everything I was supposed to do. I poured myself into my work and family, believing that if I kept pushing forward, I would eventually arrive at that elusive feeling of fulfillment. But no matter how much I achieved, how many milestones I reached, or how much financial security I built, I always felt that something was missing. I was exhausted, stressed, and constantly questioning if I was on the right path. I felt a relentless pressure to keep pushing, ignore how tired and frustrated I was, and just keep going no matter what. I had built a life that looked successful, but I didn't feel successful at all.

That's when I realized that fulfillment doesn't come from checking off a list of accomplishments or meeting society's definition of success. Fulfillment comes from alignment—from stepping into the life you were meant to live, owning your truth, and refusing to sacrifice your well-being, dreams, and desires.

Who Is this Book For?

This book is for the high-achieving, powerhouse woman who's checked every box, climbed every ladder, and achieved everything she was told would make her feel fulfilled—yet still wakes up wondering, *Is this all there is?*

It's for the woman who's led teams, built businesses, raised children, managed households, and poured herself into every role she's been assigned—only to find that in the process, she's slowly disappeared from her own life.

It's for the high-achieving, mission-driven leader who's tired of being forced into false choices: success *or* self-care, ambition *or* peace, achievement *or* joy. She knows she was made for more—but *not* more to *do*. More to *be*. More to *feel*. More to *live*.

This book is for the woman who no longer wants to perform for the world but longs to come home to herself. Who's ready to rewrite the script that says productivity is her worth and sacrifice is her identity.

It's for the woman who's ready to reclaim her energy, her voice, her time, her boundaries, and her God-given purpose. She's not looking to *escape* her life—she's ready to *elevate* it. To build a life that feels as aligned and fulfilling on the *inside* as it appears on the outside.

If you've ever thought, *I should be happier than this*, or *Why do I feel exhausted even when I'm succeeding?*—this book is for you.

The Traditional Narrative of Womanhood Isn't Working

For generations, women have been taught that caring for others is their highest calling—but while service is a vital part of a meaningful life, it was never meant to come at the expense of our health, dreams, or fulfillment. We've been taught to be the glue that holds everything together—the caretakers, the nurturers, the ones who sacrifice for the good of those around us. We've learned that our worth is measured by how much we can give, how much we can endure, and how well we can support the dreams of others while quietly silencing our own.

While service and sacrifice have their place, too many women have lost themselves in the process. They wake up one day realizing that they have spent years—sometimes decades—prioritizing everyone else's needs while neglecting their own. They are praised for being strong, selfless, and dependable, yet deep down, they feel depleted, unfulfilled, and disconnected from their true selves.

The world has celebrated the woman who can do it all, but rarely do we stop to ask if she *wants* to do it all. We don't ask if she's exhausted, if she feels alone in her struggles, or if she has dreams and desires beyond what she's been allowed to express. And when she does speak up—when she dares to say she wants more—she is often met with resistance. She's told she should be grateful. That she should appreciate what she has. That wanting more is selfish.

But what if more isn't selfish? What if it's necessary?

What if the very thing keeping women stuck in exhaustion and burnout is the belief that they must shrink themselves to be enough? When they step out and start achieving goals and dreams beyond their family life, many women feel they need to do it alone without support or that they need to hide their light or shrink back so as not to make others uncomfortable. What if we allowed ourselves to redefine success, love, energy, and purpose on our own terms? What if we sought true *fulfillment*?

Fulfillment Isn't a Destination—It's a Way of Living

One of the biggest myths we've been taught is that fulfillment is something we'll reach one day—after we hit the next milestone, after we achieve the next goal, after we have more time, money, or resources. We chase an ever-moving finish line, believing that if we just push a little harder, we'll finally feel the sense of peace and satisfaction we crave.

But fulfillment doesn't magically appear at the end of a checklist. It's not found in the next promotion, the next relationship, or the next level of success. We must intentionally create it—not just in the future, but right now.

Fulfillment is about *alignment*. It's about stepping into who you were meant to be, not just who the world expects you to be. It's about creating a life that reflects your values, desires, and purpose. Most importantly, it's about recognizing that you don't have to burn yourself out to build it.

In my journey, I learned this the hard way. I spent years hustling, striving, and doing all the "right" things, only to realize that I was constantly running on empty. I was pouring from an empty cup, convincing myself that if I could just push through, things would get easier. But the truth was, the more I ignored my needs, the harder everything became.

It wasn't until I redefined my version of success—one that prioritized my energy, well-being, and sense of fulfillment—that everything began to shift. I learned that true success isn't about doing more; it's about doing what matters. It's about having the courage to let go of the things that drain you and fully step into the things that light you up.

The Fulfilled & Limitless Framework

This book isn't just about identifying the problem. It's about creating a roadmap for real, sustainable change. The framework I share in these pages is designed to help you reclaim your energy, redefine success on your terms, and build a life that feels limitless.

The first half of this book will guide you through The Fulfilled Life Formula—a step-by-step process for breaking free from the traditional narrative that tells you how you "should" live and instead creating a life that aligns with your deepest desires. We'll cover essential elements like:

- Identity: Understanding who you truly are beneath the roles you've been assigned.
- Energy: Learning how to protect, manage, and cultivate your energy so that you can show up fully in every area of your life.
- Faith & Mindset: Building the inner resilience and belief systems to sustain lasting fulfillment.
- Love & Relationships: Creating relationships that support and elevate you, rather than drain and diminish you.
- Taking Ownership: Owning your past, present, and future with radical responsibility and intention.
- Healing: Addressing past trauma, breaking cycles, and learning how to move forward with peace.
- Growth & Purpose: Finding meaningful work and building a life that feels deeply meaningful and significant.
- Celebration & Joy: Learning to savor and appreciate the journey instead of constantly chasing the next goal.

In the second half of the book, we'll dive into **Implementation**—how to turn these concepts into daily habits and real-life changes. You'll learn how to create a personal roadmap, build sustainable habits, overcome common roadblocks, and navigate setbacks without losing momentum.

Most importantly, this book will challenge you to stop waiting for permission to live the life you want. You don't need to justify your desires. You don't need to ask for validation. And you certainly don't need to sacrifice your well-being to be worthy of the life you want to create.

Throughout the book, you'll find assessments and journal exercises to help you apply what you're learning in real time. You're welcome to complete them however works best for you—on the page, in a notebook, or online. To compliment your experience, you can download printable versions of the exercises along with a workbook, bonus tools, and resources here: www.LimitlessBookResources.com.

You Are Not Here to Play Small

Every woman has the potential to build a life that is fulfilling and limitless. But too many of us have been playing small, holding back, or settling for less than we truly desire because we've been taught that we should be content with what we have.

I'm here to tell you that **you don't have to settle.**

You *are* meant for more. Not more exhaustion, not more obligations, but more impact, more joy, more freedom, and more fulfillment.

And the best part? You don't have to do it alone.

I wrote this book because I know what it feels like to be stuck between what the world expects and what your soul truly desires. I know what it feels like to be weighed down by responsibility, fear, and self-doubt. And I also know it's possible to break free—to step into the life you were meant to live with confidence, clarity, and conviction.

This is your invitation to stop waiting and start creating. To stop settling and start stepping fully into the woman you were always meant to be.

Welcome to Fulfilled & Limitless. Your journey starts now.

PART 1:
The Fulfilled Life Formula

CHAPTER 1
The Fulfilled Life Formula

Stepping Into the Wholeness You've Always Longed For.

"Fulfillment Isn't a Destination—It's a Way of Living!"
— Christi Cossette

At some point in your life, you've likely asked yourself, **"Who am I to...?"** Who am I to start that business? Who am I to write that book? Who would listen to me? Who would buy my product? Who would ever read it?

This inner dialogue isn't unique—it reflects the conditioning that so many brilliant, ambitious women have internalized. Society tells us to be smart, but not too smart. Bold, but not too bold. Persistent, but not too demanding. Successful, but never at the expense of our family. The messaging is exhausting, contradictory, and designed to keep us questioning ourselves instead of stepping fully into our power.

But here's the real danger: if you spend your life bowing to the expectations of others—your boss, family, society—you risk losing yourself completely. You may have built an impressive career, be the go-to person in your company, and appear to "have it all together," but behind closed doors, you feel drained, disconnected, and unfulfilled.

Fulfillment isn't just about success. It's about alignment.

High-achieving women often chase success with relentless drive, only to wake up one day feeling exhausted, unfulfilled, and disconnected from what truly matters. Perhaps you have reached a point where you've checked all the "success" boxes—an impressive career, financial stability, and leadership roles yet still feel like something is missing.

That's because fulfillment isn't about how much you achieve—it's about how well your life aligns with your deepest values, priorities, and purpose. The missing piece isn't working harder or doing more—it's learning how to intentionally design a life that supports your well-being, relationships, and personal mission.

And that requires **balancing three core elements: time, energy, and priorities.**

That's where **The Fulfilled Life Formula** comes in.

The Fulfilled Life Formula

Fulfillment results from living in alignment with who you are, what fuels you, and why you're here. When your energy is protected, your purpose is rooted in faith, love, and service, and you stay committed to growth—you unlock a life that feels expansive and grounded.

$$\text{Fulfillment} = (\text{Identity} \times \text{Energy} \times \text{Purpose}) + \text{Growth} - (\text{Fear} \times \text{Burnout} \times \text{External Validation})$$

Core Elements of a Fulfilled Life

A fulfilled life isn't built by accident—it's created with intention. These four elements work together to form a life of wholeness, impact, and deep satisfaction. When these areas are aligned, you don't just *do more*—you *become more* of who you were created to be.

Identity

Know who you are beyond the roles you play and the expectations others place on you. True fulfillment starts with remembering the woman you were before the world told you who to be—and living in alignment with your core values.

Ask: Who am I when nothing is being asked of me? What do I value most deeply?

Energy

Your energy is your most valuable resource. Protecting your physical, mental, emotional, and spiritual bandwidth allows you to show up fully and sustainably for what matters most—without burning out or breaking down.

Ask: Where is my energy going—and is it aligned with what I value?

Purpose

Purpose is the integration of faith, love, and meaningful work. It's not just what you *do*; it's why you're here. It's how you live out your values, serve others, and follow your unique calling with intention and impact.

Purpose = Faith + Love + Meaningful Work

Purpose becomes the core driver of a fulfilled life—bringing clarity to your decisions and depth to your daily life.

Faith

Faith is your anchor and compass. It's the belief that you're not alone, that your life has meaning, and that there's a greater plan at work—even when things feel unclear. Faith empowers you to let go of control and trust the process.

Love

You were never meant to do life alone. Fulfillment flourishes in authentic, life-giving relationships—with your partner, children, friends, community, and yourself. Love fuels your soul and reminds you of what really matters.

Meaningful Work

Meaningful work is the expression of your purpose in action. It's the work that lights you up, aligns with your values and strengths, and allows you to make a real difference. It's not about status or striving—it's about doing what you're uniquely called to do, in a way that feels honest, energized, and deeply satisfying.

Ask: Am I living with intention, rooted in faith, guided by love, and using my work to fulfill the purpose I was created for?

Growth

A fulfilled life is built through growth and self-discovery. Growth is your commitment to expansion—mentally, emotionally, spiritually, and professionally. It's how you stay engaged, avoid stagnation, and step into your next level with clarity and confidence.

Ask: What new skills, mindsets, or habits am I building that align with my next level?

Core Detractors That Undermine a Fulfilled Life

Chapter 10 is dedicated to overcoming failure and setbacks and facing roadblocks that get in our way of fulfillment, but for now, let's focus on the core detractors.

Fear

Fear often masquerades as logic or self-protection, but underneath, it's the voice that keeps you small. It whispers, "What if I fail?" or "Who do I think I am?" and convinces you to shrink, stay silent, or hold back from your next step. Fear isn't always loud—it's often quiet and persuasive. If left unchecked, it will keep you stuck in comfort instead of walking out your calling.

> "Be strong and courageous. Do not be afraid; do not be discouraged, for the Lord your God will be with you wherever you go." (Joshua 1:9, NIV)

Ask: Where am I letting fear make decisions that were meant to be led by faith?

Burnout

Burnout is the slow unraveling of your energy, joy, and purpose. It doesn't happen overnight—it accumulates through constant output without meaningful replenishment. You tell yourself to "just keep going," but your body, mind, and spirit are waving red flags. When burnout sets in, even the things you once loved begin to feel heavy. Rest isn't a reward—it's a requirement for sustainable impact.

> "Come to me, all you who are weary and burdened, and I will give you rest." (Matthew 11:28, NIV)

Ask: Where am I pushing past my limits, and what would it look like to honor my need for rest?

External Validation

When your sense of worth depends on applause, approval, or achievement, you start performing instead of living. External validation can look like success on the outside—but it leaves you empty on the inside. You start making decisions based on what looks impressive rather than what feels aligned. True fulfillment begins when you stop proving and start choosing from a place of inner knowing.

> "The fear of man will prove to be a snare, but whoever trusts in the Lord is kept safe." (Proverbs 29:25, NIV)

Ask: Am I living for approval—or living in alignment with who I truly am and what I'm called to do?

Fulfillment is not a destination—it's a way of living that requires clarity, energy, and alignment. When these elements work together, you feel energized, clear, and fully in control of your life. When they are out of sync, you feel stuck, drained, and unfulfilled.

Many high-achieving women focus entirely on external success—career, finances, productivity—without anchoring into who they really are, what fuels them, and what really brings them meaning. This creates a cycle of burnout, where no matter how much they accomplish, it never feels like enough.

The truth is, you will never feel fulfilled if your success comes at the expense of your identity, energy, or purpose.

This book is designed to take you through each part of The Fulfilled Life Formula—starting with the foundation: who you are and what truly matters.

Because fulfillment isn't accidental—it's intentional. And the more you align your time, energy, and actions with what truly fulfills you, the more unstoppable you become.

Making Yourself the Priority

Before we begin, we need to discuss the importance of making ourselves the priority. So many women have been conditioned—by culture, family, faith, or past experiences—to believe that their worth is measured by how much they do for others. They carry the silent burden of always being available, constantly meeting needs, and endlessly giving without ever pausing to receive. The result? They are exhausted, burned out, and quietly resentful, wondering why they feel so disconnected from joy, purpose, and themselves. That kind of self-neglect isn't noble—it's unsustainable. And it's built on a lie. The lie that says you are only valuable when you're useful to others. The truth is, your needs matter. Your energy matters. You matter. When you make yourself a priority—not in a selfish way, but in a soul-honoring way—you show up more fully, more joyfully, and more powerfully in every role you hold. Prioritizing yourself is not weakness; it's wisdom. And it's the first step toward a fulfilled life.

Growing up, I was taught there were very clear roles a woman must play. Women were expected to be available to their husbands and children at all times. If they worked outside the home, it was only to contribute financially, but they were still responsible for running the household—three meals a day, a clean house, kids taken care of, etc. My mother worked full-time yet still carried the full mental load of managing everything at home. She had five kids, the first three back to back in three years, and was exhausted. She quickly gained weight and dealt with stress and overwhelm largely on her own as my dad worked long hours. She turned to food and "retail therapy" for comfort. I watched this play out in front of me. For the first 16 years of my life, she worked tirelessly to be everything to everyone and meet the demands and expectations of others. She often mentioned that she never felt rested and that no matter how hard she worked, things never seemed to get any better. She couldn't lose weight no matter how hard she tried, and the bill collectors called regularly because she couldn't keep up with the payments from all the things she bought to make herself feel better. Then one day, she died suddenly of a massive blood clot, and we were left to fend for ourselves. It was devastating for our family! I saw firsthand that being everything to everyone else at the expense of your personal wellness does NOT help anyone in the long run. Sadly, this wasn't enough to learn my lesson.

Fast forward to my life—I have a husband, three young boys (one with special needs), a full-time career, and my own business as an executive coach, author, and speaker. Doing all these things would be unsustainable if I didn't care for myself. For years, I wore overwhelm like a badge of honor. When my kids were babies, I hardly slept. I felt I had to prove I could be both a successful mom and a career woman. I felt judged by many other moms who seemed to have it all together. They put their kids first and their careers on hold. They breastfed their babies. They kept a clean home. They support. You are NOT failing as a parent. Give yourself permission to ask for the support you need so you can get the rest, nourishment, and vitality that you deserve. I've learned the hard way that running on fumes is not sustainable, it's not noble, and it's certainly not the way to reach your full potential.

High-performing women need support too. We need systems, we need help, and we need permission to put ourselves first so we have the energy and vitality to give to others. Because when we don't, we don't just suffer—our teams, families, and businesses suffer too. That's why fulfillment isn't just about success. It's about alignment. And there are **three key mindset shifts you need to make** to reclaim your energy and unlock the clarity, confidence, and capacity to lead in every area of your life.

1. Work-Life Balance Is an Illusion—Focus on Adaptability

The idea that we can perfectly balance work, family, health, relationships, and personal growth all at the same time is a myth. It's impossible, and more importantly—it's unnecessary.

The reality is that life operates in seasons. Some seasons demand more of your time at work, while others require more focus on your personal life. True empowerment comes from learning to adapt to what matters most in the moment.

If you have a high-stakes presentation, that takes priority. If your child is sick, that takes priority. Neither choice makes you more or less committed to your career or family—it means you're adapting to the highest priority at the time.

The shift we need to make isn't about "balancing it all"—it's about focusing on what truly matters and giving ourselves permission to shift gears without guilt.

2. You Must Put Yourself First, Not Last

You cannot pour from an empty cup. If you're burned out, exhausted, or running on autopilot, you cannot bring your best self to your family, career, or personal goals. The solution? Prioritizing yourself is not selfish—it's the most strategic thing you can do.

Think about it:

- Would you let your company's most valuable asset run on fumes? No. You'd invest in it, protect it, and ensure it had everything needed to perform at its best.
- **You** are your most valuable asset. If you're constantly drained, the world misses out on your gifts, ideas, leadership, and impact.

Putting yourself first means:

- Building a morning routine that nourishes you physically and mentally.
- Going to bed earlier to protect your energy.
- Drinking enough water and fueling your body with real nutrition.
- Prioritizing movement and exercise—not as an obligation, but as a way to recharge and refresh.
- Finally booking that doctor's appointment for your hormones or gut health instead of putting it off for another year.
- Scheduling time alone—whether it's a weekend retreat, a massage, or simply an hour with a book.
- Hiring help where needed—a house cleaner, a babysitter, a personal chef.
- Setting boundaries to limit access to any person who drains your energy.

- Saying no to things that drain you or don't take priority right now. Remember, saying yes to something always means saying no to something else. Make sure you spend your time on things that truly matter to you.

When you are energized, strong, and clear-headed, you don't just function better—you make better decisions, lead more powerfully, and create a greater impact.

3. Align Your Time, Money, and Habits with Your Priorities

If you want real change, you must stop letting other people's urgencies dictate your life.

Your calendar, bank account, and daily habits reflect what you truly prioritize. If they don't align with the life you want to build, it's time to recalibrate.

This requires:

- Boundaries—Learning to say no to anything that doesn't serve your highest priorities.
- Intentional scheduling—If something matters, put it on your calendar. Time-block your non-negotiables.
- Strategic spending—Investing in your growth, health, and fulfillment instead of just reacting to what's urgent.
- Consistent habits—What you do daily shapes your future. Small changes, made consistently, create massive results.

Master your day, and you will master your life.

Taking Action

This is just the beginning. You now know that fulfillment isn't about achieving more—it's about creating a life that aligns with what truly matters to you. In the following chapters, we'll break this down even further. You'll learn how to reclaim your energy, rewire your mindset, and design your life in a way that brings you real joy, impact, and freedom. Let's get started.

CHAPTER 2
Identity

Owning Who You Were Created to Be

"I will not shrink myself to fit into spaces
I have outgrown"
— Lysa TerKeurst

Why Are You Here?

Have you ever felt lost in your own life? Wondered what exactly you should be doing right now?

If you have, you're not alone. Women experience this questioning at different stages—starting a new job, navigating a career change, getting married, having children, or even facing an empty nest. Every shift in our path makes us pause and reevaluate. We wonder, am I on the right track? Is this all there is?

If no one has told you lately, let me be the one to say:

You are loved.

You are valued.

You are needed in this world.

Not for what you do, not for how much you achieve, but simply because you exist. You are already infinitely valuable, and nothing—no title, no level of success, no external validation—will ever add to or take away from that truth.

Yet, we still strive to prove our worth. Most of us were taught to dim our gifts rather than share them. Maybe you were chastised for bragging as a child. Maybe you excelled at something and lost a friend over it. Maybe you simply raised your hand in class, got the answer right, and were picked on for being a "know-it-all." The world works hard to keep us small, to keep us safe.

But what if I told you that playing small hurts all of us?

The world misses out when you don't fully step into who you were created to be. We need your voice, your ideas, your leadership. We need the business you've dreamed of launching, the book you've been meaning to write, the movement that only you can start.

The Truth About Your Power

One of my favorite quotes is from Marianne Williamson in *A Return to Love*: "Our deepest fear is not that we are inadequate. Our deepest fear is that we are powerful beyond measure. It is our light, not our darkness, that most frightens us... There is nothing enlightened about shrinking so that other people won't feel insecure around you. We were born to make manifest the glory of God that is within us."

Let that sink in: **You were born to shine.** You were created to step into your full potential. Hiding your light serves no one.

But to become who you were created to be, you must first know who you are.

Who Were You Before the World Told You Who to Be?

When someone asks who you are, what's your first response? Many women say, I'm a mom. I'm a wife. I'm an entrepreneur. But those are roles you play, not the essence of who you are. If you lost the job, the title, the relationship—who would be left? A mentor once asked me a question that changed my life. He asked me, "What did you want to be before you became who you are today?"

I wasn't sure how to answer at first. But when I got home, I pulled out my journal and started writing:

- I wanted to be a wife and mom, deeply loved and accepted.
- I wanted control over my future.
- I wanted to be respected and taken seriously.
- I wanted to lead—I've always been a natural leader but wasn't always allowed to be.
- I wanted freedom, autonomy, and personal power.
- I wanted to stop feeling small or weak.

Can you relate? Take a moment to reflect. What did YOU want to be before life happened?

Another powerful question: "What brought you joy before you had responsibilities?"

For me:

- I've always loved learning new things.
- I loved the smell of fresh rain, the sound of waves, and the beauty of flowers.
- I loved planning trips, events, and new adventures.
- I craved freedom—freedom to choose my path, my time, my life.

Think back to your sources of joy. What lit you up before the world told you what was practical?

The Battle for Identity

If you've spent your life trying to meet others' expectations—parents, bosses, or society at large—you're not alone. We're conditioned to fit in, to conform, to play the roles assigned to us.

For years, I felt like I was too much—too opinionated, too ambitious, too direct. Yet, at the same time, I felt not enough. Not feminine enough. Not quiet enough. Not what the world told me I should be.

It wasn't until I fully accepted myself that I finally felt free. I stopped waiting for permission to be who I already was.

You don't need permission either.

The Lie of "Too Much" and "Not Enough"

I hear it over and over again from high-achieving women: the persistent feeling of being both *too much* and *not enough*—often at the same time. I know that feeling intimately because I've lived it too.

As a child, I was constantly labeled:

"Too bossy."

"Too opinionated."

"Too loud."

"Too much."

I was told to sit down and let the men talk.

I was asked, "What could *you* possibly add to this conversation?"

These messages didn't just shape how I saw myself—they chipped away at my confidence. And on the flip side, I simultaneously felt like I was never quite *enough*.

Not a good enough wife.

Not a good enough mom.

Not a good enough daughter, woman, friend, or helper.

I couldn't win. I simply didn't fit the mold. And deep down, I began to believe that maybe I was broken because of it.

But I've come to realize, I'm not broken. The mold is.

The world has handed us impossible standards that constantly shift, contradict themselves, and keep us second-guessing. Society tells women:

- Be confident, but not intimidating.
- Be ambitious, but not *too* ambitious.
- Speak up, but don't be *too* opinionated.
- Be nurturing, but not weak.
- Be successful, but not so successful that it makes others uncomfortable.

We've been conditioned to edit ourselves. To shrink. To mold ourselves into someone more palatable. And it's left so many women caught in a painful tug-of-war between who they actually are and who they've been told they *should* be.

Let's call it what it is: a lie.

You are NOT too much. And you ARE enough. Exactly as you are. Right now. Without changing a thing.

The truth is, you were created with intention, with power, and with a purpose. The very traits that others tried to tone down in you are likely the ones you're meant to lead with. Your voice, vision, and strength are gifts, not flaws. You don't need to fit into someone else's mold. You were made to break it. It's time to stop contorting yourself to meet ever-changing expectations—and start stepping fully into who you were always meant to be.

Your Experiences Shape Your Calling

If you're unsure of your calling, don't start with a title or a job description. Start by looking at your life. Specifically, look at the resistance you've faced.

Where have you hit the most opposition?

What battles have you had to fight more than once?

What parts of yourself have others tried to silence or shrink?

Because *Your calling is often hidden in plain sight—disguised as struggle.*

Our culture tends to paint resistance as a sign to turn back, to play it safe, to stop pushing. But I want to offer you another perspective: **resistance is often confirmation.** It's the friction that shows you're rubbing up against something powerful—something that matters.

For me, the pattern was undeniable.

I've always been a trailblazer. A truth-teller. A bulldozer clearing the way for others to rise. And from an early age, I faced pushback. I was told I was too intense, too direct, too driven. I was urged to soften my tone, to stop asking questions, to blend in. I felt it in school. In church. In the boardroom. Over and over again, I was given the message: *tone it down.*

But here's what I've learned: **the very thing you are most criticized for is often the exact thing you're here to lead with.**

It took me years to understand that what others saw as "too much" was evidence of the strength I was born to carry. The qualities society wanted me to hide—boldness, vision, truth, power—were the exact qualities I needed to fulfill my purpose.

Your past isn't random. Your pain isn't pointless. And your resistance? It's a roadmap.

Think back:

- Where have you felt silenced?
- What fire have you had to fight to keep burning?
- What part of you refuses to die, no matter how many times it's been buried?

That may be the key to your purpose.

The enemy of your soul doesn't waste energy attacking parts of you that don't matter. He aims straight at your power, your voice, your calling. So **if you've faced resistance in a certain area, take a closer look—it may be your highest assignment.**

You weren't meant to just survive your story. You were meant to use it. Every scar, setback, and time you were told "you can't" are clues. They've been shaping you for something bigger than you might have imagined.

So don't run from the resistance. Rise in it. Your calling is not found in who the world wants you to be. It's found in who you've always been—especially in the moments when you've had to fight to be her.

You are not off course. You are being refined.

And the fire you've walked through? It's not just for you. It's so you can carry light for others who are still finding their way.

The Shift from Self-Sacrifice to Self-Leadership

But here's the tension: once we realize that our past resistance has shaped our purpose, we must confront the identity we've built in response to that resistance. For so many high-achieving women, that identity has been rooted in proving we can handle it all. We've become the one everyone counts on. The one who never drops the ball. The one who keeps it all together—even when she's falling apart inside. We've worn that identity like armor, and it's gotten us far. But eventually, that version of ourselves stops serving us. It keeps us stuck in survival mode instead of growth. And if we want to live out our true calling—not just perform at a high level, but live a life that fulfills us—then we have to do more than chase purpose. We have to adopt a new mindset. One that gives us permission to evolve. One that invites softness, support, and self-trust. One that makes room for a new identity—one rooted not in self-sacrifice, but in self-leadership.

Necessary Mindset Shifts

If you want to change your life, you *must* change your mindset first. This isn't just motivational fluff—it's backed by decades of research.

Psychologist Dr. Carol Dweck, in her groundbreaking book *Mindset: The New Psychology of Success*, introduced the concept of the fixed mindset versus the growth mindset. Her work has since become a foundational part of modern psychology, especially in education and leadership. But I believe it's even more critical for high-achieving women who are reaching a breaking point.

Here's how the two mindsets differ:

- **Fixed Mindset:** Believes abilities, intelligence, and values are static.
    - "I'm not good at that, so I never will be."
    - "This is just the way I am."
    - "If I have to ask for help, I've failed."
- **Growth Mindset:** Believes you can develop new skills, grow through effort, and improve with time.
    - "I may not be good at that *yet*, but I can learn."
    - "Every challenge is an opportunity to expand."
    - "Asking for help is part of evolving."

At a glance, it seems obvious which one to choose. But for so many high-achieving women I've coached, especially those who are the breadwinners, carrying the insurance, and managing everything at home *and* work, it's not that simple.

Why? Because we've been conditioned to survive through a fixed mindset.

We were taught that we had to be *the best*—not *get better*. We were told to be twice as good, work twice as hard, and *never let them see us sweat*.

And so we did.

We built the career.

We climbed the ladder.

We proved we could do it all.

But now, at the peak—or what was supposed to feel like the peak—we're tired. Burned out. Disconnected from joy. And often trapped in lives we worked so hard to build… but no longer love.

I've sat across from brilliant, capable women who whisper the same thing behind closed doors:

"I can't keep doing this."

"But I can't stop either—people are counting on me."

"My job provides the income, the benefits, the stability."

"I *should* be able to handle this."

So they keep pushing even when they're falling apart inside. Because admitting they need help feels like defeat.

We were never taught how to **pause, reassess, and ask for support.** We were taught to keep going—no matter the cost.

Even at home, many of these women carry the emotional and physical labor of family life. They plan the meals, manage the schedules, handle the housework, and play the role of caretaker—on top of running teams, businesses, or entire companies. Not because they *want* to do it all. But because they've been conditioned to believe they *should*… and that no one else can do it as well anyway.

- "If I hire someone, I'll have to train them. I don't have time for that."
- "If I let my husband plan the meals, we'll be eating frozen pizza every night."
- "If I stop doing it all, everything will fall apart."

Here's the shift we must make:

- **Delegating isn't defeat. It's leadership.**
- **Asking for help isn't weakness. It's wisdom.**
- **Letting go isn't failure. It's freedom.**

We've got to rewire our internal narratives. Because what's really holding many of us back isn't the workload—it's the belief that we *have* to carry it alone.

No one was meant to do life by themselves. Not at home. Not in the workplace. Not in their purpose.

You are not weak for being tired. You are not a failure for needing rest. And you are not selfish for wanting a life that *also* serves you—not just everyone else.

Many of us are living like we're doing three people's jobs—because we are. And it's why we feel stretched so thin, estranged from our families, and like we're failing at the very thing we set out to succeed in.

We need to stop. Step back. And rebuild.

Rebuild a life that supports you—not just the one that looks good on paper.

Rebuild your routines so they include rest, not just responsibility.

Rebuild your mindset so you see boundaries not as barriers, but as bridges to a better life.

You still want more—and you *should*.

You still have more in you to give—and you *do*.

But you can't serve others well from an empty, overextended place.

So let this be your permission slip:

You don't have to do what everyone else asks of you to matter.

You are allowed to make changes.

You are allowed to choose *yourself* without guilt.

And most importantly, you are allowed to believe that life can feel fulfilling again. But it starts with your mindset.

We've Been Doing This to Ourselves

Here's the hard truth—and also the most empowering one:

We've been doing this to ourselves.

Not because we're weak. Not because we're incapable. But because we *believed the lie* that we had to do it all—and do it alone.

Somewhere along the way, we internalized the message that to be taken seriously, we had to prove our worth by carrying everything ourselves. That strength meant silence. That asking for help meant failure. That needing rest meant we couldn't handle it.

So we didn't ask. We didn't stop. We didn't let go.

We took pride in being the one who always showed up, delivered, and pushed through, even at the expense of our own well-being. We wore exhaustion like a badge of honor. And in doing so, we created the very cycle we're now desperate to break.

But here's the most powerful truth of all:

If we've been part of the problem… we are also the solution.

This is not about blame—it's about *ownership*. We don't need to wait for someone else to give us permission to rest, to delegate, or to change.

We get to choose a different way.

We can choose to:

- Say no without apology
- Ask for help without shame
- Redefine strength to include softness
- Redefine leadership to include letting go
- Redefine success to include joy, freedom, and rest

You don't need to prove anything anymore. You've already done that. Now it's time to protect what you've built—and rebuild what no longer serves you.

You don't need to be saved. You need to remember your power.

You get to create a life that *feels good to live*, not just one that looks good on paper. And that begins the moment you decide that you are worthy of support, rest, and living with alignment.

So let this be your turning point. You don't have to do it all. You were never meant to. You were meant to lead wisely, live fully, and serve from a place of overflow—not depletion. That starts now. With one courageous decision: To no longer be the one standing in your own way.

Own Who You Truly Are and What You Truly Want

The question is simple—but it demands courage:

Are you living as your most authentic self?

Not the polished version.

Not the one who plays the part.

Not the one who bends and shifts to meet everyone else's expectations.

But *you*. The real, whole, unfiltered you.

If the answer is no, then it's time.

Not someday. Not when you finally "arrive." *Now*.

Because here's the truth: the world doesn't need you to fit in. It doesn't need you watered down, muted, or constantly adjusting yourself to be more acceptable or less disruptive. The world needs **you.** Fully. Unapologetically. Powerfully.

Owning who you are means:

- Telling the truth about what you want.
- Reclaiming the parts of yourself you were told were "too much."

- Letting go of the pressure to please everyone and do it all alone.
- And stepping fully into your power—even if it makes others uncomfortable.

Because when you live in alignment with who you *truly* are and what you truly want, you give others permission to do the same. Your authenticity becomes an invitation. Your courage becomes a catalyst. Your light helps others find their way.

You don't need to be more of what the world expects. You just need to be *more of who you already are. Because the real you is MORE than enough!*

So if you've been waiting for a sign, this is it.

It's time to stop performing.

It's time to stop proving.

It's time to start *becoming*.

Own your voice. Own your power. Own your truth. Own your life.

Action Steps: Aligning Your Identity

1. Journal Exercise: Write down who you were before the world told you who to be.
2. Mindset Check: Identify one limiting belief you need to unlearn.
3. Self-Reflection: Are you being fully you, or are you hiding parts of yourself?

Exercise: Values Assessment

Aligning Your Identity with Your Core Truths

Many high-achieving women have done values exercises before. You might already know your top five values—at least on paper. But if you're reading this book, something inside you is searching for more. This isn't just about naming values; it's about uncovering what's truly driving you and whether your life reflects those truths.

Values aren't just ideals we admire—they are the foundation of our fulfillment. When we feel stuck, drained, or disconnected, it's often because we're unconsciously living out of alignment with what we say we value. This exercise is designed to help you see beyond the surface and challenge yourself to reconnect with what truly matters.

Step 1: Reflect on What Matters Most

Before diving into the list, take a deep breath and ask: "When I imagine my most fulfilled, authentic self... what truly matters to me?"

Write down any words, themes, or values that surface—*without filtering or editing.*

Step 2: Identify Your Lived vs. Ideal Values

Many people list values they *aspire* to have, but the real question is: *Are you actually living them?* Below is a curated list of values across core areas.

1. Circle the values below that resonate deeply with you.

2. Star (*) the values you activity live out and embody in your daily life.
3. Underline the values that feel important, but you struggle to prioritize.

Value Categories

Achievement & Growth – Success, Learning, Challenge, Excellence, Influence, Mastery

Freedom & Flexibility – Independence, Autonomy, Adventure, Creativity, Innovation

Impact & Leadership – Making a Difference, Service, Mentorship, Legacy, Contribution

Connection & Love – Family, Friendship, Loyalty, Belonging, Authenticity, Empathy

Integrity & Character – Honesty, Respect, Fairness, Responsibility, Accountability

Well-Being & Balance – Health, Rest, Inner Peace, Joy, Simplicity, Harmony

Faith & Spirituality – Purpose, Meaning, Faith, Gratitude, Transcendence, Surrender

Wealth & Security – Financial Freedom, Stability, Generosity, Legacy, Prosperity

Step 3: Identify Your Patterns

Look over what you circled, starred, and underlined. Then answer:

- What do I notice about what I value most right now?

- Where am I living in alignment?

- Where is there a gap between what I value and how I'm living?

- Are there any values I'm ready to let go of—or reclaim?

Step 4: Choose Your Top 5 Core Values

Out of everything that stood out, pick the five values that feel *non-negotiable* for the life you're building.

My Top 5 Core Values Are:

1.
2.
3.
4.
5.

Step 5: Reality Check—Are You Living Your Values?

For each of your top five values, rate how aligned you feel (0-10) between what you say you value and how you live it.

Value	How Important Is It? (0-10)	How Aligned Is Your Life with This Value? (0-10)
1.	__/10	__/10
2.	__/10	__/10
3.	__/10	__/10
4.	__/10	__/10
5.	__/10	__/10

Step 6: Align Your Life

If there's a big gap between importance and alignment, what's causing that disconnect?

What excuses or external pressures are pulling you out of alignment?

Next to each value, write one way you can live more fully into it this week. Small, intentional action creates realignment and momentum.

Step 7: The Hard Truth—What Values Are You Prioritizing?

Forget what you *wish* you valued for a moment. If a stranger looked at your calendar, habits, and daily decisions, what would they say your true values are?

- List how you spend most of your time and energy each week (both work and personal life).

- What values do your actions reflect? Are they the ones you claim to value?

How You Spend Your Time & Energy	What Value Does This Reflect?	Does This Align with Your Core Values? (Yes/No)
_____	_____	_____
_____	_____	_____
_____	_____	_____

If your daily actions don't align with your stated values, what needs to change?

Step 8: Define Your Non-Negotiable Values

Values without boundaries are just wishes. If you say something matters to you—but regularly allow it to be pushed aside—it's time to draw a clear line in the sand.

Boundaries are the commitments you make to yourself about what you will no longer allow to get in the way—whether that's overworking, people-pleasing, or self-sabotage.

Ask yourself:

What do I need to start saying *no* to in order to honor this value?

Where am I compromising this value out of guilt, fear, or habit?

Am I willing to hold this boundary even when it's inconvenient?

For each of your top five values, define one **non-negotiable boundary** that will protect it.

Value	Non-Negotiable Boundary to Protect It
_____	_____
_____	_____
_____	_____
_____	_____
_____	_____

Example: If you say you value health, your boundary might be: "*I will not overbook my schedule to the point where I neglect sleep, movement, or nutrition.*"

Are you genuinely willing to enforce these boundaries, even when it's inconvenient or uncomfortable? If not, is this really a core value?

Step 9: Live Your Values Through Aligned Action

Boundaries protect your values. Actions bring them to life.

Now it's time to move from protection to **pursuit**. For each of your top five values, identify one **specific action** you will take to begin living more in alignment with it.

This step is about movement—choosing one small, meaningful shift that reflects your commitment to what matters most.

Ask yourself:

What's one thing I can do this week to bring this value to life?

What would it look like if I actually *lived* this value, not just named it?

Where can I take ownership and lead myself forward?

Commit to one change per value that will bring your life into greater alignment.

Value	One Change to Align with This Value
_____	_____
_____	_____
_____	_____
_____	_____
_____	_____

Example: If you say you value family, your action might be: *"I will create a weekly non-negotiable family dinner with no work interruptions."*

Owning Your Values

What's the most significant insight you gained from this exercise?

What are you ready to stop doing because it doesn't align with your values?

What's one immediate change you will make today?

Your Life Is a Reflection of Your True Values

Fulfillment isn't about *what you say you value*—it's about what you actually live. If your life feels off track, this is the moment to redefine and realign.

Are you ready to live by your true values, not just the ones that look good on paper?

> Remember you have access to a variety of assessments, journal exercises, and downloadables on the private book resources page here: www.LimitlessBookResources.com.

CHAPTER 3
Energy
Reclaiming Your Energy, Your Rhythm, and Your Power

"Your energy is your greatest currency.
Protect it like your future depends on
it—because it does."
— Anonymous

My journey of learning to prioritize my needs has been long and arduous. Beyond the issues I've already shared with wanting to please others and not standing up for myself, I've also had several health challenges that have held me back. I've learned the hard way that managing my energy is critical. I can't give what I don't have and neither can you! One of the first key lessons we must learn is to take care of our health and bodies. Women have a bad habit of giving to everyone all day, only to find, despite our exhaustion, the only few minutes we have to ourselves are late at night. So we stay up late and don't get enough sleep. We don't eat the right foods because we're always grabbing something quick and easy on the go. We often don't get the help and support we need to manage our day-to-day activities very well, so we are constantly running until the moment we fall into bed. All day we are doing that next activity, checking things off our to-do list and ensuring that everyone and everything is taken care of without ever stopping to think about whether this is working for us or serving us. In short, we deplete ourselves because we don't pause to assess how we are, or what our body needs in this moment. Usually the best we can muster is to ask ourselves, "Why do I feel so damn tired all the time?"

This is an area that I still struggle with. I was raised to "Suck it up, buttercup." This means no complaining, dealing with whatever comes your way, and no matter what just keep going. In my family, this also meant I wasn't allowed to show fear or weakness. I wasn't allowed to rest, and above all, I must never cry! I was always expected to be productive, happy, and friendly. Even though I now realize that this attitude does NOT serve me well, I am still very regularly running from one activity, task, or meeting to the next with almost no margin in my day. I often eat on the run or while in meetings. I still struggle to take breaks during the day and frequently have back-to-back meetings. But I have made progress.

I'm doing so much better than I used to. I at least schedule breaks in my day and do my best to get outside for a walk after lunch each day. Sometimes we take family walks at night. I try to eat in my kitchen instead of at my desk. I schedule date nights with my husband and regular meetups with my friends. This is about progress, not perfection.

I've learned the hard way that the ongoing narrative that we were raised with, that women are only here to support and care for others or make others happy, just doesn't work. **If we continue to put ourselves last, all we do is give our least to the ones we love.** How much more effective could we be at serving others if we had the strength, courage, and energy to make a meaningful impact?

What if?

- What if we actually had the patience and presence to enjoy time with our kids instead of feeling like we were just trying to survive the day or screaming at them in frustration because we're so tired?
- What if we stopped feeling guilty for resting and instead saw it as a necessary part of being our best selves?
- What if we had the confidence to set boundaries without feeling selfish or like we were letting people down?
- What if we weren't so depleted that we numbed out with food, alcohol, or scrolling, and instead felt fully alive and engaged in our own lives?
- What if we woke up excited for the day ahead instead of feeling like we were already behind before we even got out of bed?
- What if we genuinely wanted to have sex and then actually enjoyed having sex with our partners?

- What if we stopped beating ourselves up for all the things we didn't do and celebrated what we were able to accomplish?
- What if we actually believed we were worthy of joy, success, and fulfillment—not just for others, but for ourselves too?

In my quest to finally feel better, because I love learning new things, I became a certified health coach with Dr. Stephanie Estima's program. Dr Stephanie is amazing and has helped me so much. I first learned of her when I found her book *The Betty Body*. She is an expert in women's health and hormones. I signed up for the program because I wanted to learn to understand my own hormones and the best way to take care of my body.

It was a fabulous program, but I quickly realized that with everything else going on in my life, I didn't have the energy, stamina, or follow-through to complete the program without having someone hold me accountable. So I've been working with my own health coach, doing quarterly detoxes to support my body. I regularly take supplements, I exercise daily, and make sure that I strength train twice a week. Once I entered my 40s, I had brain fog and fatigue that didn't make sense. Despite sleeping seven to eight hours a night, I would wake up exhausted and still felt like crap throughout the day. After doing a ton of research and getting recommendations, I decided to see a functional medicine doctor who specializes in bioidentical hormone replacement therapy. I learned that I was low in testosterone, progesterone, DHEA, pregnenolone, and several other key hormones were out of balance. I gained access to a specialized compound pharmacy, and after two months, I noticed a considerable improvement in my energy and overall vitality. If you are a woman in your late 30s or early 40s and are noticing similar symptoms like brain fog, fatigue, hair thinning, low libido, etc., please find a good doctor, and get your hormones checked. This is critical to support your body as you age. In general, I want to ensure that I'm taking great care of my body so I can live a long and healthy life full of energy. My goal is to live to a very old age and see my children and grandchildren grow up. I want to live the full life that my mom didn't get to have.

Overall, we need the mindset that we matter and it's not a crime to take up space. **We are worth being taken care of!** Once we come to that realization and stop feeling guilty about taking time to care for ourselves, we begin to figure out what we need to feel better. It's not always easy. My journey has had many twists and turns, but I'm hopeful you can shortcut yours by learning from mine.

It's incredibly important to notice how we feel about things. High-achieving women often ignore their feelings to keep pushing forward, but throughout the day, I encourage you to take moments to stop and pay attention to how you're feeling. What does your body need?

I've been blessed to follow and learn from many wonderful health gurus and coaches. Whether books and courses by Dr. Stephanie Estima and Dr. Stacy T Sims, or Kristin Rowell's Energetically Efficient courses, I've learned countless tips and tricks on what matters the most to achieve meaningful results in your energy and health. Through testing various options and protocols, I've found the below health tips have had the greatest impact to my health and wellbeing. Consider these ideas, tips, and tricks on the best ways I know for women to take better care of themselves and to *feel* better inside and out. Please don't take this as another "to-do" list, but consider them experiments that you can try to see how and if they help you. Try one at a time. If you like one, keep doing it and build from there. If it doesn't make a difference, feel free to drop it and move on to a different one. These are meant to nourish and support, not dictate what's best for you. I invite you to try them out.

My Top Health Tips for High-Achieving Women

Strength Train

Strength training is one of the most powerful tools women can use to reclaim their energy, resilience, and overall well-being. Far beyond aesthetics, lifting weights builds bone density, preserves muscle mass, and boosts metabolism—critical factors in maintaining strength and vitality as we age. Resistance training also plays a key role in balancing hormones, reducing stress, and improving insulin sensitivity, all of which contribute to better long-term health. Strength training is a game-changer in preventing osteoporosis, enhancing joint health, and even supporting cognitive function. But **perhaps most importantly, lifting heavy weights builds confidence**. It teaches women that they are capable, powerful, and worthy of prioritizing their own strength—both physically and mentally. I go to a gym called Discover Strength twice a week for a full-body workout. I chose the small group option and absolutely love it! I have been going since before I had kids, and not only has my confidence skyrocketed (nothing makes you feel like you can take on the world like lifting twice your body weight on leg press!) but it's made daily activities like bringing in groceries, lifting pretty much anything, running up the stairs, carrying my kids, etc., so much easier. Strength training is my absolute TOP tip for prioritizing yourself, building confidence, and making your daily life easier. **Try it and see the difference!**

Move Daily

I'm sure you've heard this thousands of times, but nothing else will make you feel better than exercising daily. Our bodies are designed to move; when we honor that, we feel stronger, more energized, and more in control of our well-being. Moving daily doesn't have to mean intense workouts or hours at the gym—it simply means being intentional about incorporating movement into your routine in ways that feel good and are sustainable.

One of the simplest and most effective habits you can start today is **walking for 10 minutes after each meal**. Not only does this improve digestion, but it also helps regulate blood sugar levels, reducing post-meal spikes that can lead to energy crashes and cravings. I do this daily, and it's one of the easiest ways to support your metabolism while giving yourself a mental reset.

Another great way to ensure you're moving enough is by aiming for **10,000 steps per day**. You don't have to get them all at once—small increments add up. Take the stairs instead of the elevator, park farther away from your destination, or walk while on phone calls. Movement doesn't have to be structured to count. I have a standing desk with a walking pad and love to get steps in that way too. You can even set an alarm every 15 minutes and stand up, refill your water, or do 10 squats. Have a dance break or stand and stretch. Being aware and getting in movement is far more important than what the movement is.

For more intentional exercise, find something you love that you can be consistent with. I get on my **Peloton bike 3-4 times per week** for a moderate-intensity ride—not pushing to my max, just focusing on **building up a sweat** to help me **detox and support my lymphatic system**. Sweating is one of the most underrated ways to help your body clear toxins, and regular, moderate-intensity workouts are a fantastic tool for physical and mental well-being.

If cycling isn't your thing, here are other simple ways to move daily:

Strength training (even 10-15 minutes of bodyweight exercises like squats, lunges, or pushups can make a difference)

Yoga or stretching (especially helpful for nervous system regulation and stress relief)

Rebounding (mini trampoline workouts) to support lymphatic drainage

Dancing (turn on music and move—it's fun, mood-boosting, and a great cardio workout)

Outdoor activities like hiking, paddleboarding, or simply walking for fresh air and sun exposure

The key is **consistency over intensity**. You don't need to do grueling, all-out workouts every day to reap the benefits of movement. But you do need to move. Even on the busiest days, **commit to at least one small movement practice**—a short walk, stretching, or even deep breathing with intentional movement. Your body will thank you.

Get Your Hormones Checked

If you're 35 or more and feel tired or off in any way, don't accept this as normal. It may be "common" but not "normal." Get your hormones checked by a naturopath or functional medicine doctor. Based on my personal experience, most primary care physicians are trained to prescribe drugs and perform surgeries but have not been trained in nutrition or holistic remedies. Find a holistically trained doctor. I've seen far too many friends go to their primary care physician and get gaslit and made to feel like it's all in their head. Don't settle for this treatment! You deserve to feel good. Find a doctor who will work with you and get to the root of the issue vs. masking it.

If you choose hormone replacement therapy (HRT), make sure you use bio-identical hormones—here's why it matters. Bio-identical hormones are structurally identical to the hormones your body naturally produces. This means they fit into your hormone receptors perfectly, allowing your body to recognize and metabolize them just like your own hormones. In contrast, synthetic hormones (like those found in traditional HRT or birth control pills) are chemically altered versions that may not interact with your body in the same way. As always, talk to your doctor about what's right for you.

Increase Your Water Intake

Hydration is one of the most overlooked yet powerful ways to support your health, energy, and metabolism. Most women don't drink enough water; even mild dehydration can lead to fatigue, headaches, brain fog, and slowed digestion. A good rule of thumb is to drink at least half your body weight in ounces of water per day—so if you weigh 150 pounds, aim for at least 75 ounces. However, you'll need even more if you're active, sweating regularly (like during workouts or sauna sessions), or consuming caffeine. Proper hydration supports hormone balance, detoxification, digestion, and skin health. It even helps curb cravings, as thirst is often mistaken for hunger. If you want better energy, clearer skin, and improved digestion, start by increasing your water intake—you'll notice the difference quickly.

Even better, add electrolytes to your water to maximize hydration and mineral balance. Electrolytes—such as sodium, potassium, and magnesium—help your body absorb water more efficiently, preventing dehydration and supporting muscle function, nerve signaling, and energy production. Many people think they need to drink plain water all day, but without adequate electrolytes, that water can pass right through you without being properly utilized. I use **Redmond's Relyte or LMNT**, both of which provide a balanced blend of sodium, potassium, and magnesium without the sugar and fillers found in many sports drinks. Another great option is **Beam Minerals**, which offers plant-based, bioavailable electrolytes to support deep cellular hydration. Adding electrolytes to your water can help with sustained energy, fewer headaches, reduced cravings, and even better sleep—making it a simple yet powerful daily habit.

Find a Nutritious Diet That Works for Your Body

There is no one-size-fits-all diet, but the key to long-term success is finding an approach that works for your body, lifestyle, and energy needs. Whether it's Paleo, Keto, low-carb, Mediterranean, or high-protein, the best diet is the one that helps you feel strong, maintain stable energy, and support hormone balance. No matter what approach you take, protein should be a priority, especially for women over forty. As we age, we naturally lose muscle mass, making it essential to eat enough protein to support metabolism, strength, and longevity.

To maximize muscle retention and metabolism, aim for 30–40 grams of protein per meal, plus a snack or two to reach your total daily goal. This approach helps stabilize blood sugar, supports lean muscle, and promotes fat loss.

How Much Protein Per Meal?

To hit 30–40 grams of protein per meal, here's how much of each food you'd need:

- Chicken breast – 5 oz = 35g protein | 6 oz = 42g protein
- Ground beef (90% lean) – 5 oz = 32g protein | 6 oz = 38g protein
- Salmon – 5 oz = 31g protein | 6 oz = 37g protein
- Eggs – 4 large eggs = 28g protein (pair with Greek yogurt or cheese to reach 35–40g)
- Cottage cheese (low-fat) – 1.5 cups = 40g protein
- Greek yogurt (plain, non-fat) – 1.5 cups = 30g protein
- Protein powder – 1 scoop (varies by brand) = 20–30g protein (pair with a small protein snack to hit your goal)

High-Protein Snacks to Fill in the Gaps

- Beef jerky – 2 oz = 24g protein
- Hard-boiled eggs – 2 eggs = 12g protein
- Cheese sticks – 2 sticks = 14g protein
- Protein shake – 1 scoop + milk = 25–35g protein

Getting enough protein can sometimes feel like a part-time job—but at least this one comes with delicious perks. The easiest way to hit your goal is to start your day with a high-protein meal, include at least 5–6 oz of meat or fish at lunch and dinner, and add in a protein-packed snack. Stick to this, and you'll feel stronger, more energized, and more in control of your metabolism.

Manage Stress

Stress is one of the most significant hidden barriers to weight loss. For high-performing women, stress can be extremely difficult to recognize and manage. Chronic stress raises cortisol, the body's primary stress hormone, which signals your system to hold onto fat—especially around the midsection. When cortisol is constantly elevated, it can lead to insulin resistance, sugar cravings, poor sleep, and even muscle breakdown, making it even harder to lose weight despite doing "everything right."

For driven, ambitious women, stress can become so ingrained in daily life that it feels normal. I struggled immensely with this. When I had my DNA tested, I discovered that my genetics wire me for extremely high-functioning anxiety—so much so that I often don't even realize I'm stressed because it's simply my baseline. But just because I don't feel it doesn't mean it's not impacting my body, hormones, and overall well-being. I've had to be intentional about building rest and relaxation into my schedule, and I've learned that this doesn't mean putting my goals on hold—it means putting my well-being first. In fact, by prioritizing recovery, I show up better, think more clearly, and execute at an even higher level.

Some of the key practices that have helped me include:

A gratitude practice—This has been life-changing for me! I use a planner that includes both a journal and gratitude section. Each morning, I set my intentions for the day and write down five things I'm grateful for. This may sound simple, but it has completely shifted my perspective on life—I'm always looking for the good. In the evening, I check in with myself, reflect on how I did, and take a moment to savor something specific that made me happy—like my son's laugh. I pause, relive the moment, and smile.

Prayer & meditation—Grounding myself daily in faith, gratitude, and reflection.

Breathwork & deep breathing—A simple five-minute practice can instantly shift the nervous system into a relaxed state.

Daily movement & exercise—Not to check a box, but to refresh my mind and body while helping my system process stress.

Monthly massages—Releasing muscle tension helps signal to my nervous system that it's safe to relax.

Taking naps when I need them—This happens rarely given my schedule, but giving myself permission to rest without guilt, especially on weekends, is so freeing.

Personal retreats (minimum three nights alone)—These are game-changers! I sleep, nap, journal, read, dream, plan, and get massages—fully disconnecting so I can reconnect with myself and my mission.

Annual kid-free vacation with my husband—One full week at our favorite resort, completely unplugged, to reconnect and recharge.

Other great ways to lower stress include:

Journaling—Getting thoughts out of your head onto paper can help reduce mental clutter and overwhelm.

Cold plunges or sauna sessions—Both help with nervous system regulation and cortisol balance.

Spending time in nature—Walks outside, grounding barefoot, or simply getting sunlight first thing in the morning.

Laughter & fun—Watching a comedy, listening to music, dancing—anything that brings pure joy.

If we don't intentionally prioritize relaxation, our bodies will keep running on stress and storing fat as a survival response. It's not about doing less—it's about creating space to recharge so we can perform at our highest level. And ironically, when we do that, we actually achieve more, feel better, and unlock our full potential.

Eliminating Energy Vampires: Identifying and Removing Energy Blockers

While nurturing your body through exercise, nutrition, and stress management is essential, protecting your energy from external drainers—those "energy vampires" that leave you feeling depleted despite your best efforts—is equally important. These can be people, habits, or environments that slowly sap your vitality. The following sections are designed to help you identify and address these issues through reflective questions and practical steps, so you can reclaim your energy and create space for growth and joy.

Identifying Energy Vampires

What is draining your energy in the following categories?

Toxic Relationships

In Your Marriage or Partnership

Many women find themselves shouldering a disproportionate share of responsibilities at home, even when they are the primary earners. To assess whether your relationship is balanced and supportive, ask yourself:

Household Responsibilities:

- "Do I feel that household tasks—like cooking, cleaning, and meal planning—are shared fairly between my partner and me?"
- "After a long day, do I feel relief knowing my partner contributes, or do I feel solely responsible for keeping everything running smoothly?"

Emotional and Mental Load:

- "When managing appointments, kids' schedules, and daily planning, do I receive support or acknowledgment from my partner?"
- "Do I often worry about the mental burden of handling everything on my own?"

Value and Partnership:

- "Do I feel appreciated for the efforts I put into our relationship and family life?"
- "Is there clear evidence of my partner contributing financially, emotionally, and practically to our home?"
- "Can we openly discuss our roles, and are my concerns met with understanding and willingness to share the load?"

Among Friends and Social Circles

Reflect on how your friendships make you feel:

- "When I share my successes and struggles, do I feel genuinely supported, or am I met with indifference or criticism?"
- "Do interactions with friends leave me feeling energized and valued, or do they often leave me feeling drained or anxious?"
- "Are there specific friendships that consistently make me question my self-worth or decisions?"
- "Do my friends celebrate my achievements and offer a listening ear during challenges?"

In the Workplace

Evaluate the energy dynamics in your professional life:

- "Do I feel recognized and valued by my colleagues and superiors for the work I do?"
- "Is there a sense of camaraderie and support at work, or do interactions frequently leave me feeling stressed and unappreciated?"
- "Am I able to communicate my needs and boundaries openly, or does the environment discourage vulnerability?"
- "Do I experience genuine collaboration on my team, or is there an undercurrent of competition and negativity?"

Negative Environments

Consider your physical and digital surroundings:

- "Does my physical space—my home or workspace—promote calm, or does it feel cluttered and chaotic?"
- "Do I feel more drained than energized when I enter certain settings?"

- "How do I feel after spending time on social media or receiving constant notifications? Does it leave me refreshed or exhausted?"

Self-Sabotaging Habits

Reflect on your internal dialogue and behaviors:

- "Do I often engage in negative self-talk or set impossibly high standards that leave me feeling inadequate?"
- "Are there recurring patterns in my behavior, such as procrastination or perfectionism, that drain my energy?"
- "When facing challenges, do I offer myself compassion, or do I harshly criticize myself?"

Removing or Minimizing Energy Blockers

Once you've identified the sources of energy drain, consider these practical tips and strategies to help remove or minimize their impact:

Set Clear and Compassionate Boundaries:

Communicate Openly: Initiate gentle, honest conversations with your partner, friends, or colleagues about how you're feeling. Use "I" statements to express your needs without assigning blame.

Learn to Say "No": If certain interactions or commitments consistently drain you, practice declining or limiting those engagements.

Schedule Check-Ins: After meetings or social events, ask yourself, "How do I feel?" and adjust your future interactions based on your energy levels.

Curate Your Environment:

Organize Your Space: Ask, "Does my physical environment nurture calm or chaos?" Declutter or rearrange your workspace or home to create a more uplifting atmosphere.

Create a Recharge Zone: Establish a dedicated space where you can retreat to recharge, whether it's a quiet corner for meditation or a small area filled with items that bring you joy.

Implement a Digital Detox:

Set Specific Screen-Free Times: Designate parts of your day—like the first hour after waking or the last hour before bed—as technology-free.

Replace Digital Habits: Substitute endless scrolling with activities that recharge you, such as reading, journaling, or walking outside.

Prioritize Self-Care:

Daily "Me Time": Regularly schedule moments just for you—whether it's a quiet cup of tea, a hobby, or a short walk. Identify small things that bring you pleasure, and include those moments in your day or when you need a "pick me up." One of my favorite "pick me ups" is taking a deep breath of my favorite scented face oil before applying it to my face morning and night. It helps calm me and reminds me there are beautiful things in life to be enjoyed and savored. I also love keeping fresh flowers in my kitchen.

Self-Care Checklist: Create a list of daily or weekly self-care activities that help restore your energy and stick to it. You can build these in proactively or refer to the list as needed.

Seek External Support:

Lean on Trusted Allies: Whether it's a supportive friend, a mentor, or a therapist, sometimes an external perspective can provide valuable insights and guidance.

Join Supportive Communities: Surround yourself with groups—online or in person—that promote positive interactions and mutual encouragement. If you're local to the Twin Cities, consider joining The Powerhouse Women Network. Learn more on my website: www.ChristiCossette.com

By asking these targeted questions and taking deliberate steps to address the answers, you create an actionable plan to reclaim your energy. Remember, protecting your energy isn't selfish—it's necessary for being your best self. When you actively remove or minimize these energy vampires, you make space for more positive influences, leading to enhanced vitality, growth, and joy in every area of your life.

Exercise: Energy Audit

Take a moment to reflect on your daily and weekly tasks. Write down everything you regularly do in your work. Then, categorize them based on how they make you feel—energized or drained. If you notice that most of your work is depleting rather than fueling you, it may be time to reassess your role or career path.

List Your Regular Tasks:

1. _____
2. _____
3. _____
4. _____
5. _____
6. _____
7. _____
8. _____
9. _____
10. _____

Tasks That Energize You:

1. _____
2. _____
3. _____
4. _____
5. _____

Tasks That Drain You:

1. _____
2. _____
3. _____
4. _____
5. _____

Reflection:

- What patterns do you notice?
- Are you spending more time on tasks that energize or drain you?
- What small changes could you make to shift your work toward what fuels you?

If most of your tasks fall under the "draining" category, it may be time to rethink your role, delegate certain responsibilities, or explore a career shift that aligns more with your strengths and energy.

Remember you have access to a variety of assessments, journal exercises, and downloadables on the private book resources page here: www.LimitlessBookResources.com.

CHAPTER 4
Purpose

What Purpose Means and Why It Matters

"You were put on this earth to achieve your greatest self, to live out your purpose, and to do it courageously."
— Steve Maraboli

Purpose isn't something you stumble upon. It's not a title, role, or single achievement. It's a way of living—anchored in alignment, fueled by meaning, and expanded through service. For powerhouse women, purpose matters because it bridges the gap between success and fulfillment. You can have the title, income, and accolades, and still feel empty if your actions aren't aligned with your deepest truth.

Across all backgrounds, seasons, and belief systems, the things that give people purpose tend to be universal: a connection to something greater than themselves, deep relationships and love, the act of serving others, and work that feels meaningful. That's why the Purpose Formula—Faith + Love + Meaningful Work—is so powerful. It reflects the core elements that bring humans fulfillment, resilience, and legacy.

When your life is rooted in purpose, everything changes. You gain clarity, resilience, and joy. Your actions become intentional. Your relationships deepen. You no longer settle for what looks good on the outside—you demand what feels right on the inside. That's why this section walks you through the three essential elements of purpose: Faith, Love, and Meaningful Work. Each is critical in living a life of impact, alignment, and fulfillment.

PURPOSE ELEMENT 1:
Faith

The Unshakable Foundation of a Fulfilled Life

> *"When you have faith, there is no need to have all the answers. Just trust the One who does."*
> — Anonymous

The Power of Faith for High-Achieving Women

As high-achieving women—executives, entrepreneurs, leaders—we are conditioned to believe that success is a direct result of our intellect, strategy, and execution. We often rely on logic, evidence, and execution. We plan, we drive, we achieve. We are constantly solving problems, making decisions, and pushing toward the next level.

But beneath the relentless pursuit of excellence, there's a deeper question that often lingers in the quiet moments: *What am I building all of this on?*

Faith is not just a belief system. It is the unshakable foundation that gives purpose to our ambition, clarity to our decisions, and peace in the face of uncertainty. Without it, even the most accomplished among us can feel restless, disconnected, and unfulfilled.

I've built my life and career on faith. It's the one thing that has guided me through grief, uncertainty, and success alike. Faith isn't about having all the answers. It's about trusting that the answers will be revealed in time. It's about recognizing that we are not in control—but the One who is has a plan greater than anything we could imagine.

And yet, I know faith can be a complex and loaded topic. Some people shy away from it. Some reject it all together. But faith, at its core, is believing in what we cannot yet see. And the truth is, we all have faith in something.

The question is:

Where have you placed your faith?

Some put their faith in money, titles, relationships, or business success. Others in their physical appearance, social status, or personal achievements. There are so many options. Perhaps for you, it's your connections, health, intellect, routines and traditions, or self-reliance. At certain points in my life, I've put my faith in one or all of these. But what I've learned—through loss, hardship, and triumph—is that true faith is built on something deeper. My faith is built on my relationship with Jesus Christ. Why? Because He is the only thing that ever holds true in all circumstances. He never changes and He is good. Life is a gift. We don't know how much time we have, so we have to use it well. No holding back. No playing small. We're here to share our gifts with the world, and faith is what guides me in doing exactly that.

Faith is the foundation I build my life on. I don't believe in coincidences—I believe in divine wisdom, guidance, and an inner knowing that continually leads me down the right path. For example, this book was not my idea. God told me to write it. It wasn't a fleeting thought or a passing inspiration. It was a deep, undeniable pull, something I couldn't ignore. So here I am, writing this book to share my story to empower women because I was called to do it.

A Faith That Wasn't Always There

I didn't always have the faith I have today. I grew up in a small-town Lutheran church, where we showed up on Christmas, Easter, and the occasional baptism. It wasn't about belief as much as about doing what was expected. My dad wanted us to be raised in the church, but he was gone a lot for work, so it never became a real part of our daily lives. And to be honest? I hated church as a kid. In my small Midwest town, it felt more like a place for gossip and judgment than for faith and connection.

But my grandma, Marjean—she was different. She was one of the few people in my life who embodied faith in a way that felt real. She was kind, steady, and full of love, and through her, I got my first glimpse of what faith could look like.

Then, when my mom died, everything changed. I was 16, and I was angry. Of all the stages of grief, I lived in anger the longest. I was mad at my mom for leaving. Mad at the world for taking her. Mad at people for expecting me to grieve a certain way. I checked out emotionally. I went to school. I went to work. I hung out with my boyfriend because he never asked me to talk about it. Every night, I cried myself to sleep where no one could see. And every morning, I woke up and felt that crushing realization all over again—she was gone, and she wasn't coming back.

I hated feeling the heaviness of grief, the guilt of every argument we had ever had that I wouldn't be able to say sorry for, the loss of what could have been. She would never meet my husband or children. She would never see me graduate high school or college. She would miss...EVERYTHING! The anger and sadness never left. I had to be strong during the day so people wouldn't see me cry. I always got in trouble as a kid when I cried. Crying meant weakness. Crying meant judgment and ridicule. I had to hold it in. So each night, I cried alone in my room where I was safe from the judgment of others. And each morning, I'd wake up and feel almost normal for a few seconds until I remembered that she was gone. Then the grief would hit me all over again like someone had punched me in the gut. And I'd get up and carry the pain with me throughout each day.

A year after her death, near the anniversary, I hit a breaking point. I was exhausted from carrying all that pain. I knew I couldn't carry it anymore. I was sick of feeling sad and angry. So amidst my tears while lying in bed that night, I finally broke. In the darkness, I shouted, "God! If you're even real, help me! Help me understand why she's gone. Help me to stop feeling so angry. I can't do this anymore! I need you to take this from me!" And He did.

Instantly, I felt something like a huge weight physically lift off my shoulders. The crushing weight came off me, and I immediately felt a deep sense of peace. I fell asleep easily that night. It was the first night in a year that I didn't cry myself to sleep. And when I woke up, I braced myself for that gut punch of grief, but it didn't come. I was still sad. But the pain, that unbearable, suffocating pain, was gone. The weight I had been carrying—the one that had felt impossible to bear—was simply gone. I knew then that something REAL had happened. God had heard my cry and answered me. Up until that point, I had always wondered if all that God and Jesus stuff was made up to make people feel better about death. Now I knew that it was real, and I had to learn more. That was the beginning of my faith journey. It wasn't an overnight transformation. I didn't suddenly wake up a devout Christian. But I started searching.

In college, I took a world religions course. I studied Buddhism, Islam, Judaism, and other faiths. That course gave me perspective, but at the end of the day, I knew Christianity was where I felt most at home. I have spent the rest of my life (and will continue to do so) learning more and more about Jesus and learning to walk with Him, to hear His voice, and answer His call. Since then, I've experienced countless miracles personally and within my family, near misses where something horrible could or should have happened but didn't, and He has carried me through countless joys and trials. I know He can and will do the same for you…if you let Him.

Faith in Real Life: Leading with Purpose

> *"Don't worry about anything; instead, pray about everything. Tell God what you need, and thank him for all he has done. Then you will experience God's peace, which exceeds anything we can understand. His peace will guard your hearts and minds as you live in Christ Jesus."*
> - Philippians 4:6-7

One of the greatest blessings of my faith journey is that trusting my life to Jesus has given me immense peace. So many of us women live our lives reacting with anxiety or depression. We are either shameful and fearful of the past or afraid of what's coming in the future. We worry about our kids, marriage, neighbors, money, job, and if we're doing enough. We worry about whether or not we are good enough parents, if we're skinny enough or pretty enough. Does anyone see the real me? If they truly knew me, would they love and accept me? Do I matter? We are constantly reminded of all the ways that we don't yet measure up. We are regularly comparing ourselves to some higher standard that we can't seem to meet. Still, when I follow the advice of this verse to stop worrying and instead to pray about it and give it to Jesus, this works every time. I know not everyone who reads this book is a Christian, not all of you believe in God or a higher power at all, and that's OK. But I can't talk about fulfillment without talking about the peace that my faith brings me. Through the many miracles God has done for me and the challenges He has brought me through, I know He is REAL. He has been a powerful force in my life, and I don't need to be afraid of anything because He is with me. He goes before me and paves the way, and He also goes behind me and cleans up my messes. I know that I'm not going to get it right on my own. In fact, I can't do any of this alone! But with Him leading me and Him by my side and Him all around me, I am convinced I can do absolutely anything that He puts on my heart to do. So can you!

In my life, I've been through the death of my mom, the tragic deaths of two best friends, and abusive boyfriends. I've constantly been told I'm not good enough and I'll never measure up. I had pulmonary embolism and almost died (I didn't and was miraculously healed instead), I fell down the stairs and dropped my son on his head when he was a baby (he's OK), I've had a child with special needs who I was pressured to abort because my doctors believed he would be a burden and his life wouldn't have meaning (spoiler alert: I did NOT get the abortion they recommended). I've gone through seasons where every step forward seemed like a battle. But I've also been through incredible highs and unforgettable trips to places like Thailand, India, Malaysia, Greece, and Italy. I have found a phenomenal love and partnership in my marriage. I have three healthy, beautiful boys who make me proud every day. I have built a career through trial and error that I absolutely love and that allows me to use my gifts every day. I have incredible friendships, a loving extended family, and a supportive community in my church. My life isn't without its challenges, but I live fulfilled—anchored by a deep peace that surpasses all understanding.

> *"Fix your thoughts on what is true, and honorable, and right, and pure, and lovely, and admirable. Think about things that are excellent and worthy of praise...then, the God of peace will be with you. - Philippians 4:8-9*

Each of these Bible verses comes with a promise. If we do our part (pray about everything and focus our attention on good things), THEN you will experience God's peace, and THEN the God of peace will be with you.

Peace can't be underestimated! It is critical to fulfillment.

The Letter About My Mom: A Legacy of Faith

Faith has taught me so much about love, grief, and legacy. It has shaped the way I think about my mother, her life, and the impact she had on me. In 2018, I wrote a letter about her and shared it on social media. A friend found it inspiring, so I thought I'd share it here. Perhaps it will help you realize how much you matter. Here's what I wrote:

Hi friends, this has been an emotional week and year for me. My mom passed away on August 5th, 21 years ago. I'm in the thick of having three young kids—two under two, and one with special needs—which means the littles are in similar stages, so it's sort of like having twins.

Because of this, my mom is on my mind constantly, and I'm reminded each day how much I miss her and wish she were with us. On the really hard days, I think of how she survived three kids under three... how tired and stressed she must have been. How, during that time, my dad worked long hours, so she had to face much of it alone. How lonely she must have felt, and perhaps how scared and even trapped she may have felt.

I can relate to her now as I never could when I was 16—when I was young, selfish, mean, and ungrateful. I wish I could tell her how thankful I am for everything she did.

I know how hard labor is. How horrible and exhausting pregnancy and delivery feel. How much joy and sorrow your kids bring to you each day. The ups and downs, the pressure of being good enough for them and helping them to become all God created them to be—to love them for who they are rather than who I may want them to be.

I remember the sacrifices she made. I don't think she had any idea how important she was to each of us. Her absence is felt every single day by each of us... even 21 years later. Even though she's been gone longer than she was with us.

If you are blessed enough to still have your mom, please hug her tight. Tell her how important she is, how much she matters, and thank her for all the sacrifices she made.

And for moms like me who are in the thick of it—know that you matter, that you're doing a good job, and that all they need is love and your simple presence... because your absence would be devastating.

That letter serves as a daily reminder for me. My absence from my family would be devastating. I have had to live without my mother, and I would not wish that on anyone. I prioritize my health, my faith, and my family because I know how short life can be. One day, my time here will be over. I can't control when that happens, but I can control how I live the time I have left; and I intend to make it count.

What Do You Believe?

So, what are the deepest desires of your heart?

For me, it's about being happy and healthy, living a long, healthy life with my husband and our boys. It's about honoring God, making an impact, and being a woman of integrity who loves well. I want people to be treated with respect and given the freedom to grow into their potential. I want my kids to be healthy and happy with a bright future. I want to seek Jesus with my whole heart, to have peace, joy, love, and hope in my daily life; and ultimately, to get to the end of my life and hear Him say, "Well done, my good and faithful servant."

My goal is to empty myself and to get to the end of my life, having accomplished everything that God put me on this earth to do. To be a woman of integrity who loved my family well and made a positive impact on others.

Finding that level of faith and trusting the process is not easy. I've often had to hand the wheel over to Jesus, recognizing that I have no idea what I'm doing…but He does.

Thankfully, Jesus has guided me every step of the way, and He can do the same for you. Faith keeps me grounded and fuels me to keep going, no matter what challenges come my way.

Faith teaches us to prioritize what truly matters, which means living with intention, knowing that every decision we make shapes our legacy.

Faith is not just a belief. It's the foundation of a limitless life. Are you ready to build yours? I encourage you to seek something bigger than yourself because that is where true fulfillment begins.

Reflection Question:

What legacy are you building? If today was your last day, would you be proud of the life you've lived?

Exercise: Strengthening Your Faith

Faith isn't something that just happens—it's something we cultivate. If you're ready to build a life rooted in something deeper, here's how to start:

Define Your Belief System. What do you believe in and why? What anchors you when life feels uncertain?

Create Time for Spiritual Growth. Whether it's prayer, reading scripture, journaling, or reflection—make space for faith in your daily life. For me, this is quiet time spent with God each morning. I read a devotional and corresponding verses, I journal, and I pray.

Surround Yourself with People Who Strengthen Your Faith. Just as we curate our professional circles, we must be intentional about our spiritual community. I love being in small groups and doing Bible studies with my church.

Surrender Control. The hardest but most powerful step is recognizing that we are not in charge. Control is an illusion. What would change if you truly trusted that God has a plan for your life?

Live with Purpose. Faith is not just about belief—it's about action. What steps can you take today to align your life with what truly matters?

PURPOSE ELEMENT 2
Love

The Heart of a Fulfilled Life: The Power of Love in a High-Stakes Life

As a powerhouse woman, you know what it means to carry weight on your shoulders. You've spent your life building—careers, businesses, teams, legacies. You are a decision-maker, a problem-solver, a force of nature in boardrooms and beyond.

You have mastered strategy, execution, and resilience. You have pushed past obstacles that would have made others quit. You have learned to navigate the complexities of leadership, personal ambition, and high-stakes decision-making.

But when it comes to love—romantic, maternal, platonic, or self-love—things are rarely as straightforward. Love isn't transactional. It isn't something you can control, manage, or delegate. It's messy. It's unpredictable. And at times, it asks more of you than you think you can give.

For many powerhouse women, love is also complicated by the narratives we've been fed. We've been told that success comes at a price. That you can have ambition *or* deep relationships, but not both. That to be powerful, you must sacrifice softness. That love is about compromise—often at the expense of your own needs.

And yet, if you strip everything away—the accolades, the money, the influence—what are you left with? At the end of your life, it won't be the deals you closed, the promotions you earned, or the milestones you hit that define you. It will be the people you loved and the depth of those relationships.

Love, in its purest form, is not a weakness. **Love is a multiplier.**

It makes you a better leader.

It makes you a better decision-maker.

It gives meaning to everything you build.

This section is about redefining love—on your terms. It's about choosing relationships that expand, challenge, and elevate you rather than those that diminish you. It's about the courage to set boundaries, demand more, and refuse to settle.

Because love, when cultivated with intention, isn't a liability. It's your greatest asset.

Partnership: The Love That Healed Me

> "A true partnership is two whole people choosing each other again and again, not because they need to, but because they want to."
> — Brené Brown

Choosing a Partner Who Fully Sees You

For much of my life, I believed that love was something to be earned. Growing up, I was taught that a woman's role was to support, accommodate, and nurture. That strong-willed women were "difficult," and that ambition made you less feminine.

I carried this belief into my early relationships. I dated men who saw my fire as something to be managed. They told me I was too intense, too opinionated, too much. And for a while I believed them.

There was the liar who gaslit me into thinking my instincts were wrong when deep down, I knew they were right. There was the fixer who was drawn to me because of my energy and drive—yet spent most of our relationship trying to change me into someone softer, quieter, and more compliant. And there was the charmer. Slightly older than me he was sexy, confident and a bit of a bad boy. Everything I thought I wanted at the time. After my mom died he became an escape from reality. Someone who didn't want to talk about her. A shield from the pain. But he was also controlling, manipulative and judgmental. Even the socks I wore on a daily basis were critiqued and ridiculed if I didn't meet his high expectations. Life with him was walking on eggshells and hiding my light. We fought constantly for three years until the night he raised his hand to hit me and stopped himself. I left the next day.

With each relationship, the message was clear:

"You will be loved, but only if you adjust yourself accordingly."

And for a while, I played along. I tried to fit into the mold of who they wanted me to be. I dimmed my light. I softened my words. I made myself smaller. But no matter how much I bent, I was never quite right. There was always more to change, more to hide, more of myself to give away. I knew this wasn't true love.

Then I met Andy.

What It Means to Be Fully Seen

I've learned about love from many different people. One was my husband, who truly healed my soul. From the beginning, Andy was different. He was the first person in my entire life who ever truly loved me for me. He didn't want to change me like so many others.

Where past partners had been *threatened* by my ambition, he was inspired by it.

Where others had told me I was *too much*, he told me I was extraordinary.

Where previous relationships had felt like a negotiation, this one felt like home.

Andy doesn't just tolerate my drive—he loves it! When asked what his favorite thing about me is, he will immediately respond that it's my passion. Not physical passion but my zeal for solving problems, ending human trafficking, protecting the weak, raising my voice, and speaking up. Every other man I had previously dated saw my passion as intimidating, as something to be stifled. Andy knew it pointed to what matters most and that rather than have my flame be stomped out, it needed to be fanned and further ignited.

For the first time, I was in a relationship that didn't require me to shrink—and it changed everything!

Why the Right Partner Matters

Who you choose to partner with is one of the most important decisions of your life.

Your relationships directly impact your mental clarity, energy, and ability to lead. If you are in a relationship where you feel unseen, unsupported, or emotionally drained, it affects everything—including your career and the legacy you are building.

A powerful woman needs a partner, not a project.

If your relationship requires you to constantly explain, justify, or defend your ambition, you are in the wrong relationship. A true partner doesn't just support your dreams—they build alongside you.

As women, we spend so much time supporting our partners, children, family members, and friends in accomplishing all their goals and dreams. Most men, especially those in high positions, typically have a spouse and/or executive assistant who do everything from buying their clothes, cooking their meals, making their coffee, scheduling their haircuts, managing their schedule, etc. Literally handling the details of their daily lives and telling them where they need to show up and when.

While women are doing all of these activities to support their partners and families, sometimes our dreams and goals get put on the back burner. After all, who has time to change the world when you are washing dishes, folding clothes, feeding babies, meal planning, cooking dinner, scheduling all the appointments, taking your kids to soccer practice, etc.?

Having an amazing partner by your side can mean the difference between achieving your dreams or staying stagnant. I am so blessed with a fantastic man who has not only been one of the few in my life to truly love and accept me for who I am, but he has stood behind me and beside me and supported me with every goal, dream, and adventure that I have desired. He has been my biggest supporter, and I can honestly say I wouldn't have been able to accomplish half of what I've done so far without him. He's been extremely engaged with our children since they were infants. He has changed as many dirty diapers, cooked as many meals, and run as many errands as I have. After a scheduling mishap and a teary exit on my part, he now even takes our boys to their doctor appointments.

But perhaps most importantly, he has never said no to a dream of mine or said that my goals were too big. He has never held me back or pushed me down; he's only lifted me up. One time, after I achieved a really big goal and immediately started planning the next one, he pulled me aside and, concerned, asked me, "Christi, when will it be enough for you? When will you ever be satisfied?" He had mistakenly assumed that I was working toward an ultimate goal and would slow down once there. My immediate response to him was…never! I will always push the envelope and challenge the status quo. My ultimate goal is to get to the end of my life and hear from my Lord Jesus, "Well done, my good and faithful servant." To me, that means reaching my full potential and never giving up on the visions that God gives me for my future. And I'm so blessed that my man, although more content than I will ever be, is fully on board to walk beside me, to pick me up when I fall, and to encourage me to keep going when I have setbacks.

I truly hope and pray that each of you has a partner as amazing as I do. For any guys reading this, I hope you will take the time to honor and appreciate the women in your life who stand by you and help you achieve everything you have accomplished. And for the women, if you don't yet have the level of support I'm talking about, I hope that you find it. If not with your spouse or partner, then get help from a friend, a neighbor, a colleague, a nanny, a housecleaner, or whatever you need. None of us can do any of this alone. No one is a self-made man or woman.

Finding partners on your journey is absolutely critical to your success!

My hope is to empower and lift up a whole generation of women to step into their power, to say, "Yes, I CAN achieve my goals and dreams, and ask, "Why Not Me?" instead of "Who Am I?"

Let's stop holding ourselves back and get the help and support we need to keep moving forward, pick us up when we fall, and encourage us on our journey.

Cheers to your new company, your book, your family, your partner, and your future!

Self-Reflection Questions:

- Are you in a relationship where you feel fully seen, supported, and celebrated?
- Does your partner elevate you—or do they make you feel like you have to dim your light?
- Are you tolerating a relationship that drains you rather than expands you?

Christi Cossette

Motherhood: The Love That Broke Me Open

> *"Making the decision to have a child—it is momentous. It is to decide forever to have your heart go walking around outside your body."*
> — Elizabeth Stone

Motherhood isn't just an experience—it's a transformation. It cracks you open in ways you never expected. It forces you to expand in ways that challenge everything you thought you knew about yourself. I've learned so much more about love since having children. Before kids, my husband and I were selfish and often competed with each other or kept score. You got to go out with friends? It's my turn. I'll let you do this if you let me do that. It's not fair that you get to buy that unless I buy this. Looking back, I realize that life was so superficial at the time. Having children put us on the same team, sitting side by side facing challenges, sleepless nights, money struggles, etc., together vs. against each other and battling to win.

The pregnancy and birth of our second son, Mason, was perhaps one of the most powerful seasons to bring him and me together as partners. We found out that Mason had Down Syndrome when he was in utero. The doctors made a huge deal out of it and told us we needed to come in immediately. They sent us to a Maternal Fetal Medicine clinic for testing. I thought it was testing to determine his needs and how we could best support him. I was wrong.

Within minutes of our arrival at our first appointment, the doctor came in looking sad and upset, acting as if our dog had just died, and immediately offered us an abortion with no additional information other than Mason's diagnosis. Was he healthy? Apparently, that didn't matter. After we said no, they sent us to a genetic counselor who would "counsel us on our options." For over 60 minutes, they shared countless statistics on all the things that Mason would supposedly never do and all the ways he would be a "burden" to us and society at large. He wasn't a gift. He was an obligation. A burden. I'll spare you the details other than to say that at no point did the counselor offer us options. I had to ask for resources for people who decide to keep their babies, and the counselor looked annoyed and reluctantly dug through a drawer to find me a folder of pamphlets I could read "on my own time." They then passed us on to the next person to begin a flurry of tests. In that one appointment, we were asked no less than six times by six people if we wanted to kill our son. Each time we said no, they looked at us like we were crazy, and then their faces quickly turned to pity as they felt sorry for us and all we would have to "endure" if we kept him. One woman even touched my shoulder and said, "Oh, honey, I don't think you realize what a burden this is going to be on your life!" I almost laughed in her face. Oh, yes, because people have children because they're convenient. What a joke!

We finally got out of there after what felt like hours with a clear warning that we only had a few weeks to "change our minds" before it became illegal. Suffice it to say that I spent more time healing from the wounds those doctors gave me than I ever have worrying about Mason and if keeping him was a good decision. The truth is, *not* choosing him was never a thought. He is my son. We knew that God had a plan and purpose for his life and that choosing whether or not he was allowed to live was not our choice. Rather than get the abortion they recommended, we chose to trust God with our future.

Mason came into the world on August 27, 2016. Other than having low blood sugar due to my having gestational diabetes and being slightly jaundiced, he was perfectly healthy. He didn't have any of the medical issues the genetic counselor said were highly likely. He was an adorable, healthy baby. After we brought him home, I spent months crying. Not because of his "disability" but because I would hold him and feed him and see his sweet, beautiful face, and as my heart swelled with love, I couldn't stop thinking, "How could they ever think that you aren't meant to be here?" "How could they think you don't deserve to live?" "How could such a perfect and beautiful baby not be seen as valuable?" As a burden? It broke my heart!

Obviously, this story doesn't have an end...at least not yet. Mason is now eight years old. By age six, he had already achieved all but two of the milestones the genetic counselor said he would never do. He can read and write. He knows all his colors, shapes, and numbers. He can add and subtract, tell time, and count money. He can run, jump, climb, and do everything else his peers can do....he just does it much slower. It took him twice as long to crawl, walk, talk, etc. He's small for his age. He needs support with almost all his daily activities. He loses focus easily. He can do anything, but he just can't do it alone. His curiosity is ferocious, and he gets into mischief daily. He makes messes, he has no fear, he loves to spray water in the bathroom. He's also hilarious and the life of the party. He makes us laugh all the time, and his love and joy fill any room he's in. He genuinely LOVES people, and he gives the BEST hugs!

The only two milestones left that they claimed he'd never do are learning to drive and having children. We'll see. My attitude has always been that my job is to love him well. God blessed us with Mason for a reason, and I'm going to do my best to help him achieve his full potential. Thankfully, the state of Minnesota has many great resources for children with Down Syndrome, so he has been well taken care of. He gets speech, occupational, and physical therapy at school. He has a paraprofessional who works with him 1:1 throughout the day while he is in the classroom. She supports him with whatever he needs. Beyond resources, the most important piece of raising him has been our mindset. Children rise or fall to your expectations, so we expect the same of Mason as we do our other kids. We expect each to be honest, kind, helpful, and generous. To always do their best and to be contributing members of the household. He gets corrected and redirected just like his brothers. Sure, he takes longer to achieve the same results as his brothers, but he's proven that he can do anything. I am his advocate. I let all teachers and support staff know what I expect of him and them. I demand that they push him to his potential. Not more than he can handle but to push his limits. The result? He has blossomed.

Mason brings so much joy to this world. He has taught me to see the world in a whole new way. For so long, I focused on things that didn't really matter...like grades, messes, and accomplishments. I wanted my children to excel in school, sports, and team-building activities, build a strong resume, and get a good job. Having Mason has forced me to slow down. He has helped me to enjoy the little things. To seek progress, not perfection. To celebrate each milestone...like finally putting his own shoes on, finally learning to zip up his coat, finally brushing his teeth without assistance. Those things are worth celebrating. When you are forced to wait and sometimes wonder if it's ever going to happen...it makes the experience so much sweeter and richer when it does. Now we celebrate!

We now recognize that life isn't measured by accomplishments. It's not a competition. It's not about being the best, the fastest, or the smartest. Getting good grades really isn't *that* big of a deal, and messes can always be cleaned up. What matters far more than grades, milestones, and accomplishments are love, relationships, and cuddles. Also supporting each other and advocating for each other. It's learning to love the person for who they are vs. who you may want them to be. It's learning to be comfortable with being different and special...because we're *all* different and special in our own way.

I have always felt compelled to stand up for those who can't stand up for themselves. With Mason, God has blessed me with the personal experience of seeing firsthand the joys and pains of raising a child with special needs. The pains might surprise you. Based on the scary statistics I was told by the doctors, I thought the pains would be disappointment from all the things he couldn't do, the "burden" of having to take care of him his entire life, of perhaps never meeting his future children, all the expected doctor's appointments, medications, etc. But that's not how it's been at all. As parents, we LOVE our children. None of that matters. We would do anything necessary to support him because he's our son, and we love him! No...the pain came through other people. Watching them treat him differently. Seeing how low of a bar they set for him. People would either tell us he was their favorite of our kids, or they would completely ignore him. The odd looks and sometimes stares. The looks of pity. The time a private preschool wouldn't accept him unless we paid double to hire our own paraprofessional. The time he went to a very popular fitness center in the Twin Cities metro area in their childcare area and pushed a kid, they called us immediately and said they couldn't handle him. Never mind that my other son had done the same thing, and they simply put him in timeout for a few minutes. Yes, I'm talking about discrimination. I've seen it firsthand, and despite the pain, I can tell you with confidence that it has helped me love more deeply than I thought possible.

Mason's journey has taught me that love is not about keeping score—it's about standing side by side through the exhaustion, the fear, and the joy, choosing each other over and over again. We focus on presence and connection. Loving Mason has redefined everything I thought I knew about what matters most. He's taught me to slow down, to notice, to savor—and to anchor my worth in something deeper than achievement. But even with all that clarity, the tension doesn't disappear. Because while my heart is fully his (and my other children's), I'm also a woman with vision. A woman with fire in her bones to make an impact beyond my home. And that's where another deep struggle began—learning to be fully present for my family without silencing the part of me that still longs to lead, create, and serve on a bigger stage. That's the tension so many ambitious women face.

The Tension Between Ambition and Motherhood

For ambitious women, motherhood brings a kind of paradox—one that's rarely talked about with honesty. On one hand, we know that our children are the most important thing we'll ever do. Their needs, their hearts, their safety, and joy—none of it is negotiable. And yet, deep inside, there's also a pull to create, to build, to lead, to leave a mark beyond the walls of our home. The tension between showing up for your family and showing up for your calling can feel impossible to resolve.

I've always said: *I know my children will always be the most important thing I've ever done. I just don't want them to be the only thing I've ever done.*

But here's what I've learned: it doesn't have to be either/or. You don't have to silence your dreams to be a good mom. In fact, when you show up for the work that lights your soul on fire, your children benefit. They get to watch a woman living in alignment. They learn by your example that it's okay to pursue purpose, to take up space, to make a difference, *and* make dinner.

That doesn't mean it's easy. The guilt is real. The calendar gets crowded. There are seasons when you feel like you're running on empty. But instead of beating yourself up, what if you allowed space for the inevitable ebbs and flows of life and gave yourself permission to pursue *rhythm*? Rhythm allows for flow. It makes room for seasons—some that demand more of you at work and others that require your full attention at home.

Here are a few practical shifts that have helped me—and many other high-achieving women—walk this line with more peace and presence:

1. Define What "Enough" Looks Like in Each Role

You don't have to be the room mom, bake homemade cookies, and lead a million-dollar launch all in the same month. Ask yourself: *What does "being a good mom" look like to me in this season?* Maybe it's a consistent bedtime routine, tech-free dinners, or showing up fully for weekend soccer games. Be intentional about how you define success both at work and at home—and give yourself grace for the rest.

2. Time Block for Presence, Not Just Productivity

Put your family time on the calendar like you would a client call. Protect it. Honor it. When you're with your children, *really* be with them. That presence builds emotional safety and connection—even if it's just 15 fully focused minutes before bedtime. Your kids don't need you 24/7. They need you *attuned*.

3. Let Your Kids See You Work

Normalize ambition. Let your children see you preparing for a presentation, writing your book, or hosting a meeting. Talk to them about why your work matters—not in a defensive way, but in a vision-casting way. You're showing them what it means to use your gifts. You're teaching them how to dream, to build, and to serve others.

4. Ask for Help Without Shame

Don't wait for someone to notice you're drowning. Advocate for yourself. Whether it's a spouse, a sitter, a family member, or paid help—get support. You weren't meant to carry this alone. The most powerful women I know outsource without guilt. They don't equate martyrdom with motherhood. They know they are still the heart of the home, even if someone else is folding the laundry.

5. Reframe Guilt into Gratitude

Guilt tells you that you're falling short. Gratitude reminds you why you're showing up. Instead of, *"I feel bad I'm working late,"* shift to, *"I'm so grateful I get to do work that matters and still come home to the people I love most."* Your mindset is what creates peace, not your to-do list.

6. Know That Your Legacy Is Both

One day, your children will look back and remember how you made them feel. And they'll also remember how you showed up in the world. Your legacy isn't just in what you build professionally—it's in who you become while raising the next generation. What if your greatest achievement is raising children who watched their mother live with purpose?

We weren't meant to fragment ourselves. You can be fully mom and fully woman. Fully leader and fully nurturer. Fully ambitious and fully present.

There will always be trade-offs. But when your life is rooted in *values* rather than *obligations,* you'll know when to say no, when to step in, and when to step back. You'll know that success isn't about achieving more but about living in integrity with what matters most.

So, to the woman torn between her passion and her people—take a deep breath. You're not failing. You're growing. You're expanding. You're doing holy work in your home *and* the world. Both matter more than you know.

Self-Reflection Questions:

1. How do I define success in this season of life—both as a mother and a woman with goals and dreams?

2. Does my current schedule reflect that definition?

3. Where do I feel the most guilt when it comes to motherhood or work?

4. Is that guilt rooted in truth or unrealistic expectations?

5. In what areas of my life am I trying to do everything alone?

6. Where could I ask for help or release control without sacrificing what matters?

7. What does *being present* look like for me with my children?

8. Am I offering them quantity of time, quality of time, or both?

9. What's one practical boundary I could set this week to better honor both my family and my calling?

Friendship

Finding Your Tribe & Building Expansion Partners

> *"I would rather walk with a friend in the dark, than alone in the light"*
> — Helen Keller

The Higher You Climb, The Lonelier It Can Feel.

Success is often celebrated as an individual journey, but you were never meant to do it alone. And yet, many powerhouse women find that the more they achieve, the more isolating the journey becomes.

The friendships that once felt natural begin to feel strained. Conversations that used to flow effortlessly now feel out of sync. The people you once confided in seem to no longer understand the weight you carry—or worse, they resent it.

Why? Because as you evolve, not everyone is meant to evolve with you.

For years, I found myself clinging to friendships out of loyalty rather than alignment. I had friends who had been part of my life for years, but they seemed uncomfortable with my growth instead of excited.

I'd share a big win, and they'd change the subject.

I'd talk about my ambitions, and they'd make a sarcastic remark.

I'd mention a goal, and they'd list all the reasons it wouldn't work. It was subtle, but it was there. And for a long time, I ignored it— because letting go of friendships is painful.

But here's what I finally had to accept:

Not everyone is meant to walk every chapter of your journey with you. And that's okay. The friendships that serve you at one stage of life may not be the friendships that will carry you into your next level of expansion. You don't have to cut people off with hostility, but you do have to be intentional about who you allow into your inner circle. Your friendships should be fueling your growth, not dimming your light.

How to Build Your Tribe

If you don't have the kind of friendships that expand and inspire you, it's time to be intentional about finding them.

Because powerful friendships don't happen by accident.

They are built with purpose.

1. Seek Out Women Who Challenge You

The best friendships aren't just supportive—they push you to grow.

If you're the most ambitious person in your circle, that's a problem.

You need women in your life who:

- Inspire you to think bigger.
- Call you out when you're playing small.
- Hold you accountable to your potential.

These are the women who won't let you settle.

The ones who will tell you, *"You're playing it too safe. Go bigger."*

The ones who will remind you of who you are when you start to doubt yourself.

The ones who don't see your success as a threat but as motivation to level up alongside you.

If your current circle doesn't include women like this, find them.

Where?

- High-level mastermind groups.
- Networking events where serious women gather.
- Exclusive communities for ambitious entrepreneurs and executives.

Put yourself in rooms where women are already operating at the level you aspire to.

2. Be Willing to Initiate

Powerful friendships don't just happen—you have to cultivate them.

That means reaching out first.

A lot of ambitious women struggle with this. We assume that if someone wanted to connect, they would have already made a move.

But here's the truth:

Most powerhouse women are just as busy, ambitious, and selective about their energy as you are.

If you see a woman you admire, don't wait—start the conversation.

- Send her a message on LinkedIn.
- Introduce yourself at an event.
- Invite her to grab coffee or join a mastermind call.

If you want deep, meaningful connections, you have to be proactive about building them.

3. Let Go of Relationships That No Longer Serve You

Not every friendship is meant to last a lifetime.

Some are meant for a season.

Some are meant for a lesson.

And some are meant to stay with you forever.

But one of the biggest mistakes high-achieving women make is holding on to friendships out of guilt or nostalgia rather than alignment.

If a friendship feels like:

- A constant energy drain.
- A one-sided effort.
- A place where you feel unseen or misunderstood.

Then, it's okay to step back.

You don't have to make it dramatic.

You don't have to have a painful conversation.

You simply create space.

Because the right friendships—the ones that truly support your growth—will never require you to sacrifice yourself to maintain them.

Expansion Partners

Leveling Up Through Strategic Connections

A tribe is important, but expansion partners are next level. These are not just friends. They are not just supporters. They are collaborators, thought partners, and accountability powerhouses who actively help you grow. The concept of expansion partners goes beyond casual friendship—it's about intentionally aligning yourself with women who challenge you to elevate your game.

How to Identify & Cultivate Expansion Partners

Expansion partners are women who:

- Operate at a high level in their own right. They aren't just successful—they are actively pushing boundaries and setting new standards in their industries.
- Are deeply committed to personal and professional growth. They are not content with staying the same—they are constantly evolving.
- Believe in collaboration over competition. They don't see your success as a threat—they see it as a shared win.

These are the women who will:

- Introduce you to game-changing opportunities.
- Offer honest, unfiltered advice that pushes you out of your comfort zone.
- Strategize with you on how to scale your business, leadership, and impact.

Unlike traditional friendships, expansion partnerships require intention and strategy. Here's how you build them:

1. Be Generous First

Expansion partnerships are built on reciprocity.

Instead of approaching a connection with *"What can I get from this person?"* ask:

"How can I add value?"

- Can you introduce them to someone in your network?
- Can you offer insight on a challenge they're facing?
- Can you collaborate on something that benefits both of you?

When you lead with generosity, you attract high-caliber relationships.

2. Make Room for High-Level Conversations

Expansion partnerships require depth.

This is not about small talk—it's about game-changing conversations.

Instead of talking about surface-level updates, have discussions like:

- "What's the biggest challenge you're facing in your business/career right now?"
- "What's one thing you're working on that excites you?"
- "Where do you feel stuck, and how can I help?"

High-level women don't have time for meaningless connections—they value real, results-driven relationships.

3. Meet Regularly & Set Intentional Goals

The best expansion partnerships have structure.

Instead of waiting for a random coffee date, schedule regular check-ins.

- A monthly mastermind call to share wins, challenges, and goals.
- A quarterly strategy session to review progress and set new milestones.
- A co-mentorship approach, where you hold each other accountable for execution.

The key? Consistency.

Powerful relationships require ongoing investment—but when done right, they will pay dividends in every area of your life.

Build Your Inner Circle with Intention

You are the average of the five people you spend the most time with. So choose wisely.

Surround yourself with women who inspire, challenge, and elevate you.

Let go of relationships that keep you small, exhausted, or unseen.

Most importantly, become the kind of friend, leader, and expansion partner you want to attract. Because when powerhouse women come together with intention, they don't just change their own lives—they change the world.

Love Of Self

Boundaries As a Form of Self-Respect

> *"You are the one you've been waiting for."*
> — Byron Katie

Too many women believe that setting boundaries is selfish. We've been conditioned to accommodate, to smooth things over, to be nice—even at the cost of our own well-being. But here's the truth: **Love without boundaries is not love—it's self-abandonment.**

If you find yourself constantly explaining, defending, or justifying your needs, that's a sign that boundaries are needed.

For years, I tolerated relationships that drained me—family members who overstepped, friendships that felt one-sided, work environments that demanded more than they gave.

I told myself it was easier that way.

That I didn't want to create conflict.

That I could handle it.

But avoiding confrontation is not love—it's self-neglect.

The greatest act of self-love is teaching people how to treat you.

And sometimes, that means saying: *"No more."*

Earlier in my career, I was working in operations at a large organization and was asked to transition into a new position to bring a customer perspective into the technology space. The leader I was asked to work with was known for having a difficult personality and fostering a toxic environment. My assignment was clear: help her, model what real leadership looks like, shift the culture, and improve the team's performance.

I invested two years on that team. The toxic environment was intense. As an example, my team members would work hard on a presentation, and our leader would review it ahead of time and say everything looked fine. Then, when they presented it in a meeting, she would yell at them in front of everyone. She'd say things like, "This is terrible," or "I'm embarrassed that my team produced this," or "I can't believe you brought this garbage to a presentation." And again, this was after she had already approved it!

Situations like this happened almost daily. I tried coaching her through these issues, but she refused to acknowledge any of it or take ownership. After all, I was her subordinate. She didn't feel she needed to listen to me or take my advice. Eventually, I went to HR. They didn't take any action because she was "good at getting stuff done." So I started going to every meeting to shield my team. When she would get upset, I would interrupt, apologize, thank her for the feedback, and say we'd take it back and make changes. I constantly tried to calm the situation and protect my team from being berated.

My mentor had seen me go through this for nearly two years. One day, I explained to him what I'd been doing and said, "I really want to leave, but I feel like my team needs me to protect them." And he looked at me and said, "Oh, that's so sweet—so you're the battered wife staying for the kids." I gasped. "Oh, my God," I said. "That's exactly what I'm doing."

It hit me then—I had to leave. I was no longer helping; I had become part of the problem, not the solution. So I found a new job and told the truth about why I was leaving. Everyone else who had left before me had said it wasn't about this leader—they claimed it was about more money or a better opportunity. Most people were afraid to burn a bridge. But I felt compelled to be honest. I said, "I've coached, I've guided, I've done everything you've asked me to do. I went to HR. Nothing changed. I can't keep doing this."

It was a really hard time. Some people were angry with me. They believed I made them look bad. Maybe I burned a bridge. I hoped that, eventually, my team would understand that I was trying to help them navigate that difficult culture—not make it worse. But at the time, I didn't know what the outcome would be. Two months after I left, that leader was fired. They did an investigation and confirmed everything I had shared.

Looking back, I realize that by leaving, I was modeling something just as important as I had tried to model while I was in the role. I was modeling a boundary. I had done everything I could—I coached, I advocated, I escalated, and I stood in the gap for my team. But eventually, I had to lead myself. I had to get out of a toxic environment and show others that it's not noble to stay in dysfunction at the cost of your own well-being. Sometimes, the most powerful example you can set is to walk away. Not in anger or bitterness, but in clarity—saying, I've done all I can here. This is no longer healthy. And I value myself enough to choose differently.

It was a painful season—and a hard but necessary lesson to learn: sometimes, despite your best efforts, you can't change the system. All you can do is say, I'm not willing to put up with this. I value myself more than this. And it's time to go.

And now, I want to turn this back to you. Where in your life have you normalized dysfunction? Where have you convinced yourself that it's your job to protect everyone else while quietly sacrificing your own peace? Where are you telling yourself it's not that bad, even though every part of you is drained and depleted?

We do this as women—especially as high-achieving women who know how to endure, who know how to fix things, who believe we should be able to change it. We stay in jobs, relationships, dynamics, and environments far longer than we should because we feel responsible. Because we don't want to hurt anyone. Because we believe that if we just try harder, we can make it better.

But sometimes, the most courageous, leadership-defining act is to walk away. To say: I've tried. I've given my best. And now, I need to lead myself forward.

You don't need permission to create a boundary. You don't need to justify why you no longer want to tolerate what's unacceptable. You don't have to wait until you're completely burned out to say, Enough.

Leaving that role wasn't just about saving myself. It was about modeling a new path forward—for my team, my peers, and now, for you. If no one else has said it to you yet, let me be the one:

- You are allowed to leave.
- You are allowed to choose peace over chaos, clarity over confusion, respect over toxicity.
- You are not meant to stay small or silent to keep others comfortable.
- You are not responsible for carrying the weight of dysfunction on your back.

You are responsible for leading yourself first. And sometimes, leading yourself means walking away from what no longer aligns with who you are and what you deserve.

That is not weakness. That is wisdom.

That is not quitting. That is choosing yourself.

And that is both self-leadership and self-love.

How to Set Boundaries Like a Powerhouse

Recognize where you are tolerating less than you deserve. If a relationship leaves you feeling depleted, it's time to assess why.

Decide what you will and won't accept. You don't have to justify your boundaries to anyone.

Communicate clearly and directly. No need for over-explaining—keep it simple: *"This is what I need. If that's not respected, I will disengage."*

Enforce your boundaries unapologetically. A boundary is meaningless if you don't uphold it.

Self-Reflection Questions:

- Where in your life are you tolerating less than you deserve?

- Who in your life drains you instead of energizing you?

- What boundaries do you need to set to protect your energy and joy?

Exercise: Redefining Love on Your Terms

If you want to cultivate powerful, fulfilling relationships, you need a strategy.

Step 1: Audit Your Relationships

Make a list of the five closest people in your life.
- Do they elevate you?
- Do they challenge you to be better?
- Or do they subtly make you feel small?

Step 2: Have the Hard Conversations

If something isn't working, address it.
- That means talking to your partner about what you need.
- That means setting clear expectations in friendships.

That means saying *no* to relationships that drain you.

Step 3: Set Boundaries & Enforce Them

Decide what you will and won't tolerate. And stick to it.

Step 4: Surround Yourself with Expansion Partners

Actively seek out relationships that challenge and inspire you.

Step 5: Prioritize Self-Love

You can't pour into others if you are running on empty.

Self-care is not selfish—it's a necessity.

Love Is the Lifeblood of a Fulfilled Life

Faith is the foundation. Identity is the anchor. But love?

Love is the force that gives everything meaning.

It's the connection that makes success feel worthwhile.

It's the strength behind every risk you take.

It's the depth in your relationships, the joy in your journey, and the legacy you leave behind.

The world will tell you that love requires compromise, that you must choose between ambition and connection, between strength and vulnerability.

But you know better.

Love—when chosen wisely and cultivated intentionally—amplifies everything you build. It strengthens, fuels, and expands you.

So be bold in how you love.

Be unwavering in the standards you set.

And never settle for relationships that make you feel smaller than you were created to be.

Because at the end of your life, it won't be the titles, milestones, or bank accounts that matter. It will be who stood beside you, who you lifted up, and who you loved fiercely along the way.

Christi Cossette

PURPOSE ELEMENT 3
Meaningful Work

The Power of Meaningful Work

Most of us spend the majority of our waking hours working. That's why our work matters so much—it plays a significant role in our overall fulfillment.

And yet, far too many powerhouse women—women who are brilliant, capable, and deeply driven—find themselves stuck in roles that look impressive on paper but feel empty in their souls.

You've checked the boxes, climbed the ladder, and delivered results. You've been the go-to, the rock, the one who always gets it done. But at some point, the grind begins to feel hollow. You start to wonder: **Is this really it? Is this all I was made for?**

The truth is, we are not meant to spend the best hours of our days—and years—doing work that drains us, silences us, or asks us to shrink who we are. We are meant to do work that **lights us up**. Work that uses our talents, aligns with our values, and contributes to something bigger than ourselves.

Meaningful work is not about chasing titles or proving your worth. It's about doing work that reflects your identity, purpose, and power. It's about making an impact you can feel—not just in the company's bottom line, but in the lives you touch, the culture you shape, and the legacy you leave.

And here's the most important part: **Meaningful work doesn't just fulfill you—it fuels you.**

It taps into your creativity, voice, and vision. It becomes a source of energy instead of exhaustion. When you are doing work that is aligned with who you truly are, everything changes. You become more confident, more magnetic, more alive. You stop surviving your days and start shaping your life.

So if your work no longer reflects your calling, your values, or your full potential—it's not a sign of failure. It's a signal. A sign that you are being invited to rise, realign, and reclaim the meaning behind what you do.

But what makes work meaningful anyway?

Meaningful work aligns with your identity, connects deeply to your values, uses your unique gifts, and serves a higher purpose.

What Makes Work Meaningful for Powerhouse Women

1. Aligned with Purpose, Not Just Performance

You've proven you can hit the numbers and drive results. But at this stage, it's about more than outcomes—it's about impact. Meaningful work aligns with your **purpose**: it lets you use your voice, influence, and experience to drive change that matters to *you*.

Fulfillment isn't found in checking boxes—it's found in knowing your work changes lives.

2. In Service of a Bigger Vision

Powerhouse women want to build something that outlasts them. Whether it's a legacy, a movement, or a mission-driven company, meaningful work contributes to a vision larger than status or salary.

You're not here to play small—you're here to leave your mark.

3. Freedom to Lead Authentically

After years of adapting to expectations, meaningful work feels like *freedom*. It's the ability to lead, create, and show up as your **whole self**—without apology. No more shrinking, code-switching, or self-silencing.

When you're leading from your truth, you're unstoppable.

4. Room to Grow While Honoring Your Life

Meaningful work fuels your growth *and* respects your humanity. It challenges you intellectually while allowing space for your family, health, and dreams outside the boardroom.

You don't have to choose between ambition and well-being. You get to have both.

5. Genuine Connection and Respect

At this level, you're no longer interested in tolerating toxic cultures or performing to be accepted. You crave work that includes **collaboration without competition**, support without strings, and rooms where you're not the only woman—but one of many rising together.

Being in the right room changes everything.

6. Ownership, Not Just Responsibility

You've carried the weight for everyone else—now you want to build your own table. Meaningful work gives you **ownership**: creative freedom, decision-making power, and the chance to shape what's next.

Responsibility without authority burns you out. Ownership energizes you.

7. Recognition That Reflects Your True Value

You're done settling for being underpaid, overlooked, or under-acknowledged. Meaningful work comes with compensation, respect, and visibility that reflect your **true worth**—not just what the market says, but what you *know* you're capable of.

You're not asking for too much—you're finally asking for what's aligned.

I've had jobs where I felt like just a cog in the machine, making rich people richer. But when I zoomed out and saw the bigger picture, I realized I could find meaning in almost anything.

For example, when I worked at a prominent financial services firm, my job was to support financial advisors. It wasn't just about supporting the company but helping people build their financial futures to support their families, retire comfortably, and give generously. That broader perspective made my work meaningful.

Another example is my work in financial operations—an area many see as boring or unimportant. But I see it differently. Without accurate billing and timely collections, a company can't survive. Employees don't get paid, products don't get delivered, and businesses shut down. When you see the *ripple effect* of what you do, it changes everything.

One of the most pivotal moments in my career was when I worked as a senior leader overseeing a struggling financial process. The company had millions of dollars tied up in delayed payments, and the inefficiencies in the system were putting strain on employees and customers alike. It would have been easy to dismiss this work as just another corporate financial process, but I saw it differently. I saw it as an opportunity to transform the business, improve lives, and stabilize a struggling system. I poured my energy into solving these problems, and in the process, I not only optimized the company's cash flow but also created a healthier working environment for my team.

When you find *purpose* in your work, you don't just do your job—you change lives.

How can you shift your perspective to uncover deeper meaning in the work you already do?

Purpose: Big and Small

Purpose doesn't have to be a grand, lifelong mission. You can find purpose in small, daily moments.

I find purpose in:

- Raising my children and helping them navigate life's challenges.
- Mentoring and growing my team—helping them step into their potential.
- Building and Nurturing The Powerhouse Women Network, a space where high-level women support each other.
- Having a strong, committed marriage and setting an example for others.
- Advocating for children with Down syndrome through my involvement with Jack's Basket, a nonprofit with a mission to celebrate babies with Down syndrome.

Finding purpose is about recognizing the impact you have, no matter how small. It's about seeing the bigger picture in everything you do.

How does the value you create in your work ripple out—shaping your company's success, influencing the people around you, strengthening your community, and leaving a lasting impact on the world?

If you can't find purpose in what you're doing, **it might be time to create it.**

If You Can't Find It, Create It

I've always had a very strong personality and was very leadership minded. From a young age, I was regularly told to sit down and shut up. I was regularly told I was "too much," yet I always felt like I wasn't enough. I didn't fit into the traditional role I was told a girl should play. I was too strong-willed, too opinionated, I didn't sit still, and I had big dreams that my parents and friends thought were ridiculous. Does this resonate with you? What do you do when you don't fit in and you haven't found your people yet?

I started just trying to prove myself, so I earned an undergraduate degree and a master's in finance. I spent the first decade of my career in traditional finance roles, eventually moving to operations and then technology. I am most lit up by solving complex problems and driving major transformations to solve key business challenges. I feed on ambiguity and love a good challenge. I want to drive IMPACT in everything I do!

I worked my way up to executive leadership, leading a team of 100 people within an organization that was struggling to get customers to pay. They hired me to improve cash collections, improve billing accuracy, and optimize the entire Order to Cash process. I absolutely LOVED the work. I loved my team, I loved solving complex problems, and I loved working cross-functionally with others to resolve issues end-to-end across the entire process. It was a blast.

However, I found that the higher I went, the lonelier it got as a female in leadership. I was surrounded by men who didn't understand the unique challenges of being a woman who was managing the mental load of both work and home. None (or few) of them had to worry about meal planning and grocery shopping, scheduling doctor and dentist appointments for their family, or, in some cases, even managing their own calendar. They had a wife, mom, or executive assistant to do everything for them. Heck, some of them even had their coffee and lunches delivered. I needed the same support.

On top of the grueling schedule and other demands, my travel increased dramatically. At its peak, I was traveling three weeks a month and missed my family terribly. How could my work be fun and fulfilling but also draining and exhausting? I knew what I was doing wasn't sustainable long term unless I made some shifts. There had to be a better way. There had to be someone I could talk to about this. But my close friends, although fantastic, didn't understand what I was going through. They shared messages like "Why don't you just quit? It's not worth it. You need to use this time to focus on your family. Your kids are only young once, you know."

Yet I wasn't ready to walk away. The work filled my cup in so many ways. There had to be other women who understood what I was going through and faced similar challenges.

Since I couldn't find what I needed, I created it. I launched The Powerhouse Women Network in January 2024 with a new passion for supporting women as they navigate the top of the corporate ladder or run their companies. Being a woman operating at a high level is truly a unique place to be. As they say, it can be lonely at the top. This rings even more true for women. Historically, women have competed with each other and, in some cases, even pulled others down to "get ahead" rather than supporting each other. Yet attitudes are shifting. Women are realizing they don't have to choose between their goals and passions and their families. They just need the same level of support that men have benefited from all along.

My vision for The Powerhouse Women Network (PWN) is to connect powerhouse, badass women who are doing "it all" however they define it. These are women operating at the highest levels and navigating unique challenges.

We:

- Support each other.
- Celebrate each others' wins.
- Connect on a deep level.
- Have the honest conversations no one is talking about.
- Make introductions to other leaders who can help them grow in their life and business.

Some topics that come up:

- Being one of few women in the boardroom.
- Marital issues that arise when you are the breadwinner, or when your spouse may feel disempowered or less valued.
- Getting the help necessary to support the household when we have to travel or work late for a big project.
- Imposter syndrome—this doesn't end no matter how high we climb.
- How to find and keep great team members.
- And many more!

Most of all, I want to be around other like-minded women who "get me" and don't question why I'm always pushing for more. They already understand that it's because I know I can. They know that I feel not only called to but COMPELLED to keep moving forward because I need to reach my full potential and model the way forward for others. They understand this because they feel it too.

I'm super passionate about this topic because every woman I've met has a dream, a goal, a passion in her heart that, for one reason or another (I'm too old, too young, too thin, too fat, not pretty enough, I need to wait until my kids are older, my husband gets his master's or gets promoted. The list goes on.) has been put on hold or delayed or questioned. It's a societal difference where women are taught from a young age that they need to help everyone else, not to selfishly focus on their own dreams.

I believe the opposite. I believe that each of us MUST share our gifts and dreams with the world. We owe it to others to bring it into being because when women reach for their dreams, they ALWAYS have others' well-being in mind.

WOMEN WITH MONEY AND INFLUENCE CHANGE THE WORLD. Plain and simple.

They rebuild communities, give millions to charities, build companies that solve key challenges, and they empower others to do the same. This work is vital to the future of our world! We must!

Yet, I don't want to spend my time convincing women to step into their power and achieve their dreams. Instead, I want to show them that it can be done and come alongside the women who are already doing it so we can lift each other up, much like boats in a harbor that all rise together.

My goal on this planet is to model the way forward, inspire people to reach their full potential, and step out and do scary things so others can see that it can be done.

I make a point to do the hard and scary things like writing a book, starting a company, traveling to exotic places, and perhaps most importantly, to own and work on my stuff (my pain, my fears, past trauma, and my limiting beliefs).

I do this to build my own fulfilling life and help other women do the same. I want freedom, joy, and passion in my daily life. Don't you? That only comes by overcoming the self-doubt that asks, "Who am I to do ____?" and instead respond to that still small voice inside that asks, "What if I did the thing? What if I can? How could I change the world?"

If you feel like you haven't found your place yet, maybe it's because you are meant to create it.

Reflection Questions:

- What have you been looking but can't seem to find? Is it time to create it?

- What steps can you take to create what's missing?

Taking the Next Step

If you've realized your work is no longer fulfilling, **it's time to pivot.**

- Identify what's no longer working.
- Define what you want instead.
- Take small steps toward a life and work that align with who you are.

Your gifts, talents, and passions are not random. They are clues to your purpose.

Action Steps

Commit to Growth: Choose one book, podcast, or course to start learning something new.

Evaluate Your Work: Do an energy audit and fulfillment gap assessment.

Define Your Vision: Write down what you want your life to look like in five years.

Take One Step: Identify one small action you can take today.

Find Community: Surround yourself with people who support your growth.

Remember you have access to a variety of assessments, journal exercises, and downloadables on the private book resources page here: www.LimitlessBookResources.com.

Own Your Purpose. Live It Fully.

Ultimately, purpose isn't a destination you arrive at. It changes and evolves based on the seasons in your life. Purpose is the deep inner alignment that comes from building your life on faith, rooted in love, and expressed through meaningful work. When you live with purpose, you stop chasing external validation and start anchoring your life in what truly matters. You prioritize peace over performance, alignment over approval, and impact over image. You don't need to earn your worth—you already have it. Your job is to live like you believe it.

The truth is, a fulfilled life isn't just about what you achieve—it's about who you become along the way. Faith reminds you that you're never alone and are guided, supported, and held—even in the darkest moments. Love teaches you that you were never meant to do life alone and that powerful relationships are your greatest asset. And meaningful work ensures your gifts don't go to waste—they become the legacy you leave behind. You don't need permission to live this way—you just need the courage to choose it.

So if you've been waiting for a sign that it's time to step into your calling, this is it. You were created with purpose, for a purpose. It's time to own it, live it, and let it ripple through every part of your life. The world doesn't need more women who are burned out, boxed in, or playing small. The world needs you—fully alive, fully aligned, and fully lit up from the inside out!

CHAPTER 5
Growth

Never Settle

Never Stagnate

Live in a State

of Becoming

"You are one decision away from a completely different life."
— Mel Robbins

Growth isn't about a sprint to the finish line; it's a steady, intentional process of becoming who you were created to be. The challenge is finding the flow—pushing forward toward something meaningful without feeling like you're drowning in the urgency of getting there faster.

Fulfillment is built in the small, consistent steps you take every day. It's about trusting that the progress you're making, however incremental, is enough. You can be ambitious without being overwhelmed, driven without being consumed. Growth happens in the space between where you are and where you want to be—it's not about forcing the pace but allowing yourself to evolve, little by little, in a way that feels aligned and sustainable.

Where You Are Today Is OK

Before diving into the elements of personal growth, I want you to take a deep breath and remind yourself: that *where you are today is OK*.

You are not a failure. You are not stuck. You are not behind. You are exactly where you need to be in this moment. This isn't about achieving perfection, which is impossible and not worth striving for. Growth happens little by little, day by day.

Fulfillment is not a final destination; it's a way of living. It evolves as we do. You may find purpose in one thing today, and in five years, it could shift entirely. And guess what? That's completely okay. You have permission to change your mind at any time.

The key to living a fulfilled life is adopting a *growth mindset* that keeps you open to possibilities, learning, and change. At any moment, something could happen that shifts your entire trajectory. The question is: *are you ready for it?*

It's OK to Change Your Mind

Before we dive in, I also want to make it clear that in any area of your life, it is absolutely OK to change your mind! It's *expected*, actually. One of the most powerful things you can give yourself permission to do is change your mind. You are not locked into the choices you made yesterday, last year, or even a decade ago. Fulfillment isn't a fixed destination—it's a dynamic, evolving experience. If something no longer serves you, if a goal that once excited you now feels heavy, or if you realize you're chasing something that no longer aligns with who you are becoming, you are allowed to pivot. Growth isn't just about pushing forward; it's also about knowing when to shift, adapt, and choose a different path.

Many high-achieving women reach a point where they realize they've built a life and career that no longer serves them. When this happens, don't despair. You are right where you need to be. The solution is as simple as changing your mind. Changing your mind isn't quitting—it's self-awareness. It's recognizing that you are constantly evolving, and with that evolution comes new desires, perspectives, and priorities. You owe it to yourself to pursue what truly lights you up, not just what you once thought would. Give yourself the grace to course-correct without guilt, knowing that every change in direction is simply another step toward a life that feels deeply fulfilling and aligned.

Personal Growth: How Are You Investing in Yourself?

So let's dive in. Growth doesn't happen by accident. It requires intention. You don't have to overhaul your life overnight. Growth happens through small, consistent steps. The most fulfilled and successful people share one key trait: they never stop learning.

They don't just "fit it in when they have time." They actively set aside time each week to learn and grow.

For me, learning has always been a passion. I devour books, listen to podcasts, take courses, and join coaching programs to expand my thinking. I even budget financially for personal development courses and conferences because **investing in yourself is one of the best financial decisions you can make.**

Some options to actively pursue growth:

Growth in Knowledge & Creativity:

- Reading books that challenge your mindset.
- Listening to podcasts that inspire you.
- Taking online courses to expand your skill set.
- Starting a side project, blog, or personal brand to build new capabilities.
- Finally take up that hobby you've been daydreaming about, like painting, gardening, dancing, photography, etc.

Growth in Business

- Hiring a coach or joining a mastermind.
- Attending conferences or networking with like-minded people.
- Shadowing someone you admire or asking for informational interviews.
- Learning a new technical skill (data analysis, design, a software platform, etc.).
- Traveling to new places and immersing yourself in different cultures.
- Taking an improv class to build confidence and spontaneity.
- Practicing vulnerable conversations to deepen relationships.
- Mentoring someone else—it often teaches you just as much.

Growth in Health & Wellness

- Engaging in therapy or somatic healing work to process past wounds.
- Hiring a personal trainer to start strength training
- Incorporating daily movement into your schedule
- Hiring a health coach to find a nutrition program that works for you.

Growth in Relationships

- Asking for feedback from your partner, trusted peers, or leaders to identify blind spots.
- Practicing active listening without interrupting or jumping in with solutions.
- Learning your partner's or child's love languages—and consistently speaking them.
- Creating phone-free, distraction-free blocks of time with your family.
- Planning regular one-on-one time with each child or intentional date nights with your spouse or partner.
- Seeking marriage counseling or parenting coaching proactively—not just in crisis.
- Praying together with your family or incorporating shared spiritual practices.
- Having deep conversations with people who challenge your assumptions.

Personal Growth: Taking Ownership

As high-achieving women, we're skilled at leading teams, making decisions, and driving change in our organizations. However, when it comes to our personal lives, it's easy to slip into passive patterns, where we allow circumstances, people, or past experiences to dictate how we feel or act. The key to true empowerment is taking full ownership of your life, not just in the boardroom but at home and in your relationships.

When you fully own your decisions, actions, and outcomes, you step into your power. You stop looking outward for reasons why things aren't working and instead ask yourself: *How did I contribute to this situation? What can I do to shift it?*

The Subtle Ways We Play the Victim

As powerful as we may be in our professional lives, many of us still fall into subtle patterns of victimhood. It's not always about complaining or whining; it's about how we think and react to the challenges we face. These patterns might be more difficult to identify because they're deeply ingrained, but they can show up in various forms:

Shifting Blame: When something doesn't go the way we expected, it's easy to think, *"This person dropped the ball,"* or *"The system is broken."* While external factors may play a role, we often overlook the fact that we played a part in the situation. Did we set clear expectations? Did we communicate effectively? How might our actions or decisions have contributed?

Avoiding Tough Conversations: Many women at the executive level struggle with confrontation. Whether it's with a colleague, a partner, or even a child, we often avoid difficult conversations because we don't want to upset the status quo. But avoiding these conversations only perpetuates the victim mentality—because we're not taking ownership of the situation and addressing the problem head-on.

People-Pleasing: Even the strongest women can fall into the trap of people-pleasing, especially when managing relationships or making compromises at home. Saying yes to things that don't align with your values or needs is a form of letting others dictate your life.

When we prioritize others at our own expense, we give up our power.

Not Setting Boundaries: In your professional life, you likely have clear boundaries with your time and energy. But at home or in personal relationships, boundaries can become blurred. Whether it's over-committing to social events, constantly answering work emails during off-hours, or allowing people to treat you in ways you don't deserve, not setting boundaries is a subtle form of playing the victim.

Taking Ownership: A Mindset Shift

When facing challenges, it's easy to think about all the external factors that might have contributed to the situation. The truth is, circumstances are often outside our control. However, what *is* within our control is how we respond and what actions we take moving forward.

Here's how I process challenges:

Recognize the Outside Circumstances: First, I consider the external factors that might have contributed to the situation. This helps me gain perspective and separate my emotions from the facts.

Remember What I Truly Want: It's crucial to remind myself of my ultimate goals. Whether it's a peaceful home life, a thriving business, or healthy relationships, remembering what I genuinely want helps me refocus and stay aligned with my purpose.

Consider My Options: Once I'm clear on what I want, I think through all the possible options to move forward. What are the potential outcomes of each choice? What's the price I'm willing to pay for each option?

Take Responsibility for My Role: This is where the real ownership comes in. I ask myself, *How did I contribute to this situation?* Did I communicate clearly enough? Did I set proper expectations? Could something I said or did have been misinterpreted? Am I avoiding the tough conversations that need to happen?

Decide on Action: Once I've reflected on my role, I decide on my next steps. Sometimes, that means apologizing or having a tough conversation. Other times, it's about accepting the situation as it is, walking away, and learning from it.

The truth is, we are always building our future with every decision we make. Whether it's the relationships we nurture, the jobs we take, how we raise our children, or the people we spend time with, every action is a vote for what we want. We are constantly building something, so make sure it's something you truly want.

The Price of Ownership

Ownership requires a price. The price may be emotional—having tough conversations or confronting uncomfortable truths. The price may be practical—setting boundaries and enforcing them, even when it's hard. But the price of not owning it is far greater. When we avoid ownership, we stay stuck in patterns that don't serve us, and we forgo the possibility of growth and change.

Remember, if you're the problem, you're also the solution. When you step up to take ownership, you are also stepping into your power. You stop blaming external circumstances and take charge of how you respond. You begin to create the life you've always wanted.

Practical Steps for Taking Ownership

Here are some actionable steps to help you take ownership of your life:

Identify Areas Where You're Playing the Victim: Reflect on the areas of your life where you feel stuck or frustrated. Are you blaming others? Are you avoiding difficult conversations or decisions? Identify these patterns so you can address them head-on.

Set Clear Boundaries: Establish what you will and won't accept from others. This applies to your time, energy, and personal space. Protect your boundaries at all costs.

Have the Tough Conversations: If there's something you've been avoiding, whether it's apologizing, asking for what you need, or confronting a miscommunication, take action. The longer you wait, the more power you give to the situation.

Own Your Decisions: In every decision you make, from professional choices to personal relationships, ask yourself: *Am I making this choice based on what I truly want?* If the answer is no, re-evaluate and decide if you need to adjust your course.

Embrace the Growth Process: Accept that growth often comes from discomfort. You won't always get it right, but as long as you own your role and make conscious decisions, you'll be on the right path.

Stay Open to Feedback: Be willing to listen to feedback, even when it's hard to hear. Use it as an opportunity to learn and grow. Feedback is essential for self-improvement and can provide valuable perspectives you might not have considered.

Have the Tough Conversations

Here's a story in my own life where I had to have a challenging conversation with my husband. Owning your dreams means ensuring you have the support you need from the people closest to you. But what happens when that support isn't automatically there, especially when your partner's fears clash with your aspirations?

How do you navigate a situation when your spouse or partner, who should be your biggest cheerleader, is instead feeding your doubts?

This is exactly what I faced when I began building my business. My husband has always been a supportive partner, but when I transitioned from a steady paycheck to building my own company, the uncertainty around finances triggered his fears. Those fears began showing up in our conversations, and instead of providing the encouragement I needed, he was questioning everything I was trying to do.

I started hearing things like, "That won't work," "That's too expensive," "We need you home more," and "We can't afford that since you don't have a steady paycheck." When I mentioned considering hiring help, he would immediately respond, "We can't afford it." And when I explained my vision, he asked, "How is this different from what any other woman has done?" or "What if you don't make any money doing this?" or "This sounds like a lot of work. When are you going to spend time with me and the kids?"

These comments frustrated me. I was upset because it felt like his fear was overriding the belief that this could work. I was already battling my own fears about this new chapter, and the last thing I needed was to feel like I wasn't getting his full support. I understood his concerns—they came from a place of wanting to protect us—but I needed him to shift his thinking. I needed him to help think through *HOW* this could work, not question *IF* it was possible.

That's when I knew we needed to have a tough conversation. I couldn't let this tension go unresolved. I needed him to understand how important his support was and call him out on what I felt was unrealistic thinking. I told him, "You're asking me to make a lot of money without investing in resources, hiring anyone to help me, and putting in the time necessary to make this work. That's not realistic, and it's not fair."

I continued, "I believe God has called me to do this, and I trust that He will provide for us. But I can't do this alone. I'm already dealing with my own fears about the unknown. I need you to believe in this with me. I need you to stop leading with fear and instead think about **how** we can make this work."

I went on, "You need to start thinking of these services as investments, not expenses. Instead of saying, 'That won't work,' ask, 'How can we make this work?' Instead of saying, 'We can't afford that,' ask, 'How can we afford it? Who can we ask for help? What would we need to make this happen?'"

Then, I told him, "I'm afraid that if this doesn't change, we'll grow apart and ultimately end up divorced in a few years. We need to be aligned on this. This isn't a job for me; it's a calling, and I need to know—are you going to get on board or not?"

It wasn't an easy conversation, but it needed to happen. After several days of reflecting on what I said, he came to me and thanked me for being honest. He admitted it had been hard to hear, but he was grateful I'd said it. He told me he had spent time thinking about it and was sorry for how he'd reacted. He said, "I'm always going to choose us, and I am on board with your dreams. I believe this is God's call for you, and I need to get on board with that belief too. I trust that God will provide for us, and I'll support you every step of the way."

That moment of honesty and clarity allowed us to realign. It wasn't just about me getting what I needed—it was about coming together as a team and ensuring we were both on the same page. We had a tough conversation, and through it, we both gained a deeper understanding of what it would take to move forward **together.**

If you're in a similar situation where your partner isn't immediately on board or is focused on fear and doubt, this conversation can serve as a model. Challenging conversations like this are an opportunity to express your needs, realign your priorities, and ensure that both partners are committed to supporting each other's dreams. It's not about blaming anyone; it's about moving forward with clarity and a shared vision.

What Happens When Your Partner Doesn't Respond How You'd Hoped

In the ideal scenario, after a difficult conversation, your partner is aligned with your vision, ready to support your dreams, and willing to move forward together. But what if, after expressing your needs, your partner still doesn't offer the support you were hoping for? What if they say they're not on board with your goals or don't believe in your dreams?

It's important to recognize that this situation isn't a failure—it's an opportunity for deeper reflection and communication. If your partner says they won't support your dreams, this is a chance to pause and take stock. You might need to dig deeper into the "why." Is it fear? Lack of understanding? Different values? Or perhaps they are projecting their own insecurities onto the situation?

In this case, it's important to own your role in the situation and approach it with a mindset of understanding and resolution. Here's how to navigate the conversation:

Clarify Your Needs and Why They Matter: If your partner isn't on board, it may be because they don't fully understand how important this is to you. Reaffirm the reasons why your dreams matter. Express that it's not just a passing desire but something that aligns with your purpose, values, and even the future of your family. Make sure they know how much their support means to you and why it's vital to the health of the relationship.

Dig Deeper into Their Fears: If they're unwilling to support you, take the time to really listen. Understand the root cause of their concerns. Are they worried about financial stability? Do they fear losing your time or attention? Is there underlying resentment or a lack of trust? Digging deeper into their fears can help open up a more productive conversation where both sides feel heard and understood.

Seek a Middle Ground: If they still won't support your dreams outright, explore the possibility of a compromise. Can you adjust your approach so they feel more comfortable with it? For example, if financial security is a major concern, can you propose a plan to start the business part-time while maintaining stability? Finding a middle ground can help ease the tension while still allowing you to pursue your dreams.

Decide What You're Willing to Accept: This is the hardest part, but it's crucial. If your partner's lack of support isn't rooted in a misunderstanding or fear that can be worked through, you might need to evaluate what's at stake. Can you still pursue your dreams without their support? If not, what will you do to ensure your relationship remains healthy while you continue your journey? This may mean having further conversations, seeking external support (like therapy), or reevaluating your long-term alignment.

Own Your Dreams, Regardless: Ultimately, you are responsible for your dreams. If you're committed to making them a reality, you must take ownership and move forward with or without full support. You'll have to manage your fears, doubts, and challenges. Your journey will require strength, resilience, and, at times, tough decisions. But remember—no one can take your dreams away from you unless you allow it.

If your partner does not come around after these efforts, you don't have to abandon your dreams. While it may cause strain in your relationship, your path is still yours to walk. And you'll need to decide whether your dreams are worth fighting for, no matter what.

In my coaching practice, I've unfortunately seen this scenario too often. Sometimes, my clients have made the hard choice to walk away. This was usually when they realized their values weren't aligned with their partner; they had been settling for a lack of support for a long time and recognized the relationship would no longer work. You have the power to choose your future either way!

Personal Growth: Facing and Overcoming Trauma

Releasing the Past to Step into Freedom

Trauma is something we don't always realize we carry, yet it shapes our beliefs, our behaviors, and even our bodies. I've spent much of my life pushing through pain, telling myself to *"suck it up and keep going."* That worked—until it didn't.

For years, I wondered why I couldn't lose the weight I had gained after having three kids. I was doing all the right things—eating healthy, working out—but my body refused to let go. It wasn't until recently that I learned the real reason: my body was still holding onto the trauma of those pregnancies and deliveries, each of which had been incredibly difficult. I had heard the phrase *"The body keeps the score,"* but I hadn't truly understood what that meant until I started working with a trauma therapist.

I want to share my experience—not because I have all the answers, but because I want you to know you're not alone. If you've experienced deep pain, from childhood wounds, past relationships, loss, or even the stress of always being the one who holds everything together, it's time to release it. **You don't have to carry it anymore.**

How I Started Healing

For much of my life, I have sought healing through Sozo inner healing sessions. Sozo, developed by Bethel Church in Redding,

California, is a Christian-based technique that focuses on identifying and breaking free from limiting beliefs, generational trauma, bitterness, unforgiveness, and even spiritual oppression. This method has been profoundly effective for me, and I've used it to release countless mental, spiritual, and emotional blocks.

I've also tried traditional therapy, but for a long time, I struggled to find a good fit. Often, when I brought something to a therapist, they would tell me it was a "big deal" and would take years to work through. That never sat well with me—I wanted to heal and move forward, not spend a lifetime revisiting my pain.

Then, I found a trauma-informed therapist who changed everything. She integrates EMDR (Eye Movement Desensitization and Reprocessing), somatic work, and inner healing, and within just a few sessions, I started seeing massive breakthroughs.

The Moment I Understood My Trauma Was Stored in My Body

One of the most eye-opening realizations was that my body had been carrying trauma in ways I never recognized. I had spent my whole life pushing through discomfort—ignoring hunger, exhaustion, even the need to go to the bathroom—because I had learned early on that my needs weren't a priority.

Growing up, I didn't feel safe emotionally or physically. I had a caregiver who would react with physical punishment if I didn't do what they wanted. I learned to suppress my feelings because expressing them could get me hurt. If I cried, I was told, *"Stop crying, or I'll give you something to cry about."* So I hardened myself. I became strong, independent, and self-sufficient. I built walls, believing that if I didn't let anyone close, I couldn't be hurt again.

But what I didn't realize was that my body *never forgot*. The fear, the suppression, the need to protect myself—it all stayed locked inside me. Over time, my body responded by **holding onto weight, keeping me "safe" by creating a physical barrier** between me and the world.

My therapist helped me recognize these patterns. Through EMDR and somatic work, I started uncovering the deep-seated beliefs that had been running in the background for decades:

> *If I'm weak, I'll be attacked.*

> *If I show my emotions, I won't be safe.*

> *If I rest, I'll be letting people down.*

> *My body has failed me. I can't even do the basic functions of being a woman like carrying a baby to term.*

> *If I were a real woman, I would have been able to breastfeed and provide food for my baby.*

In short, I was blaming myself and my body for things that were completely outside my control. I had to shift my thinking from "my body is my enemy" to "my body is my partner."

Breaking Free: Learning to Listen to My Body

Once I understood this, everything changed. I had spent years ignoring my body's signals, but now, I started asking: *What does my body need?* Instead of punishing myself for feeling exhausted, I rested. Instead of numbing with food or shopping, I learned to self-soothe in ways that actually nourished me.

If this resonates with you, I want to encourage you: **your trauma is not just in your mind—it's in your body, too.** And healing is possible. I encourage you to find a trauma informed therapist who is trained in EMDR. It can be life changing!

The Hardest Lesson: Overcoming Abuse and Finding Forgiveness

Healing from trauma isn't just about releasing what's stored in the body—it's also about **letting go of bitterness and injustice.**

For a long time, I didn't think I could forgive. There are moments in life when the betrayal is so deep, the pain so consuming, that forgiveness feels impossible. It's one thing to work through your own wounds, but when the trauma involves someone you love—your child—it becomes a different kind of battle.

I have never known rage like the rage I felt when my son Mason was hurt by someone I trusted. I wanted justice. I wanted revenge. I wanted something to make it right.

But justice never came. And I was left with the weight of my own anger.

The Weight of Betrayal

I had been struggling to find reliable childcare for my two youngest sons, Mason and Preston. They were both under age two and finding a daycare that had two openings for children that were young and wouldn't cost more than my mortgage was extremely difficult. My previous daycare had closed with only a two-week notice so I was very short on time and a bit desperate. After touring almost every daycare in my town, I thought I had finally found a solution—an in-home daycare close to my house, run by a warm and loving woman. She had been a nurse and was opening her home after having her second child so she could stay home with her kids. Her husband seemed kind and gentle, and the house felt safe. The boys were happy. I was so thankful for my good luck to find them!

After a few months, I noticed that she continued to add more children to her daycare...and she seemed more and more tired and stressed with each additional child. Then, one day, something felt...off. She seemed extremely overwhelmed and definitely exhausted. I thought to myself that maybe I should start looking for other care as I didn't know if she could handle it. I had one of those gut feelings that I should pull the boys out and find other care. Something wasn't right. But I ignored it. I told myself I was overreacting. Where else could I find care for two babies under age two anyway? Especially with such short notice. I told myself to stop reading into things and that it would be fine.

Then, only one week later, Mason came home covered in bruises.

I confronted the caregiver immediately. She blamed Mason, claiming he was out of control and had hit and scratched himself, and those marks were self-inflicted. But I knew better. Mason was only two years old, a tiny little boy with Down syndrome who had never shown signs of self-harm before. Her story didn't make sense.

I reached out to a group of moms who had children with Down syndrome, posting a picture of the bruises and asking if anyone had seen something like this. The response was unanimous: That's a slap mark on his face. Those bruises are from being beaten. You need to take him to the ER. NOW!

That night, I sat in the hospital, my heart racing as doctors examined my baby. The next day, we went to Child Protective Services (CPS), where they ran more tests. I prayed that maybe, somehow, this was a mistake.

But then, the CPS agent walked in with the results.

Mason's bruises weren't random. They had a pattern—marks on his face, hips, and ribs that showed he had been beaten. His highchair had been knocked over with him in it. He had been slapped, hit, and thrown down so hard that CPS said he should have had permanent damage.

I remember hearing those words: Your son was beaten.

I sobbed. I shook with fury. I couldn't breathe.

This woman—this monster—whom I had trusted had beaten my baby. Even worse, I had been warned and ignored it. This was my fault!

The Injustice That Almost Consumed Me

CPS shut down the daycare immediately. Parents were called and told to pick up their kids right away. I was assured she would never be allowed to open a daycare again and that no one else would get hurt. But what about justice for my Mason? When it came to criminal charges? Nothing happened.

Why? Because her husband was home at the time, and the police couldn't prove which one of them had hurt Mason. She and her husband both claimed that Mason had done it to himself, and despite being interrogated separately, they stuck to their story. No one would be charged since the authorities can't charge two people for the same crime.

No arrests. No trial. No justice.

I was livid. I was vengeful. I wanted them to hurt the way they had hurt my baby. Family and friends offered to slash their tires, to throw bricks through their windows. Part of me wanted to. I envisioned starting their house on fire, keying their cars, or worse.

I wanted them to suffer. I wanted their lives to be torn apart the way they had torn apart mine. But they walked away with nothing more than a shut-down daycare and financial struggles. And I was left with something much heavier—the weight of my own rage.

The Battle to Forgive

Every Sunday, our family would drive past their house on our way to church, and every Sunday, my body would react. My chest would tighten. My jaw would clench. I would grip the steering wheel so hard my fingers would ache. My body was still carrying the trauma.

And then I heard God whisper: You have to forgive them.

I did not want to forgive them. They didn't deserve it. They weren't sorry. Every time I looked at Mason, I would cry, thinking about what it must have been like, how scared he must have been, and why I wasn't there to help him. How could I have put him in that situation?

But here's the truth about forgiveness:

Forgiveness isn't about letting them off the hook— it's about setting yourself free.

> "And when you stand praying, if you hold anything against anyone, forgive them, so that your Father in heaven may forgive you your sins." - Mark 11:25

I realized that my anger wasn't hurting them at all—it was hurting me. In fact, it was tearing me apart. Forgiving them didn't mean excusing what they did. It didn't mean forgetting. It meant refusing to let their actions hold me captive any longer.

I had to **forgive myself** for not listening to my gut.

I had to **forgive the system** for failing us.

I had to **forgive them**—even when I didn't want to.

Releasing the Weight of Trauma

As of this writing, Mason is now eight years old. It's been over six years since it happened, and I still have to forgive them regularly. We moved houses so I no longer have to drive by that house (which helps immensely), but I still dread the idea of ever running into her.

Some days, I pray for them through gritted teeth. But I pray because I refuse to let their actions poison my heart.

I find peace knowing that Mason is now safe. I remember the day after the incident, when I put him in his car seat, and he started sobbing—terrified that I was taking him back to that house. I gently grabbed his shoulders, held his sweet face between my hands, and declared:

> "Sweetheart, we are NEVER going back there. She will never hurt you again. You are safe now!"

Almost instantly, he calmed. I hugged him, buckled him in, and off we went to CPS.

Mason is safe now. And so am I.

What I Want You to Take from This

We all have trauma that tries to hold us hostage. Maybe yours isn't the same as mine. Maybe it's a broken relationship, a betrayal, a painful childhood, or the deep grief of something that should have been different.

But you **cannot carry the weight of that pain forever**.

At some point, you have to release it—for your own sake.

I hope that as you read my story, you ask yourself:

- What pain am I still holding onto?
- Who do I need to forgive—even if they don't deserve it?
- How is my body carrying the weight of this trauma?

Forgiveness doesn't mean forgetting. It doesn't mean that what happened was OK. **It means choosing to let go so that you can live freely.**

The body keeps the score, but you get to decide when the game is over.

Action Steps to Start Releasing Trauma and Letting Go of Bitterness

If you feel like your body is holding onto trauma—from childhood, relationships, betrayal, or loss—you don't have to carry it forever. Here are tangible steps to start your healing journey:

1. Seek a Trauma-Informed Therapist

Find someone trained in EMDR, somatic experiencing, or other body-based therapies to help release stored trauma.

2. Schedule a Sozo Inner Healing Session

If you are open to spiritual healing, consider a Sozo session. Sozo is a Christian-based inner healing method designed to break off limiting beliefs, generational trauma, and emotional wounds. If you're in Minnesota, I would highly recommend Dare to Believe in Burnsville, MN, which is where I go. They can be reached at dtbmn.org/sozo

If you're outside Minnesota, here is a resource to find a Sozo ministry in your area: BethelSozo.com/book-sozo

3. Practice Body Awareness

Ask yourself: *What do I need right now?* Notice where you hold tension. Place your hand on your heart or stomach, and take deep breaths to reconnect with your body.

4. Try the Color Visualization Exercise

Close your eyes, take two – three deep breaths, and imagine a color that represents comfort or healing. Picture it flowing into the part of your body that feels tense or heavy. Visualize it releasing pain or bringing warmth and safety.

5. Move Trauma Out of Your Body

Activities like yoga, walking, dancing, or shaking out your limbs help move stuck energy. Trauma often gets "frozen" in the nervous system, and movement helps release it.

6. Speak Forgiveness Out Loud

Even if you don't feel it yet, say the words: *"I choose to forgive."* Keep saying it until your heart starts to believe it. Forgiveness is a practice, not a one-time event. I've often been told that forgiveness is like a bell. Once you ring it, it doesn't just stop ringing. It takes time for the ringing to stop.

6. Process Through Writing or Prayer

Journaling about past experiences or praying for healing can help emotions surface and bring clarity. If you struggle to forgive, pray for the willingness to forgive.

7. Write a Letter You'll Never Send

Pour out all your anger, grief, and frustration onto paper. Then, rip it up or burn it as a symbol of releasing that pain.

8. Release the Need for Justice

Ask yourself: *What will holding onto this anger cost me? If justice never comes, will I let it steal my peace forever?* Hand it over to God—because some battles are not yours to carry. Do this as often as is necessary until peace returns.

You Are Worth the Healing

Know this: **your pain is valid, but it doesn't have to define you.** No matter what you've been through, you are not broken beyond repair. Healing is possible. You are worthy of feeling safe, loved, and whole.

Trauma may have shaped you, but it does not have to hold you captive. When you start releasing it—through therapy, movement, prayer, or simply learning to listen to your body—you begin to step into a new level of freedom.

And that freedom? **It's yours for the taking.**

CHAPTER 6
Living For Something Bigger
Service, Impact, and Fulfillment

"If not me, who? If not now, when?"
– Emma Watson

Up to this point, we've focused on what it takes to **build a life of fulfillment for yourself.**

We've explored:

Loving yourself fully—setting boundaries, honoring your energy, and living unapologetically.

Creating strong relationships—choosing the right partner, building friendships that elevate you, and making sure the people in your life support your highest potential.

Balancing motherhood and ambition—ensuring that you never lose yourself while also giving your family the best of you.

Rooting in faith—building a foundation of trust, peace, and divine guidance.

Doing meaningful work—aligning your career and contributions with your purpose.

Healing your past—releasing limiting beliefs and stepping fully into your power.

Reclaiming your identity—remembering who you are and living in alignment with your truth.

And many more.

And if you stopped here, you could live a **deeply fulfilling life.** Loving yourself, loving your family, and creating a life that feels aligned with who you are—**that's already a massive achievement.** But for powerhouse women like you, **there's another level.** Because at some point, fulfillment for yourself is no longer enough.

You start asking bigger questions:

What am I building beyond myself?

What impact am I making that will outlive me?

How can I use my success to create opportunities for others?

That's when you realize:

True fulfillment doesn't stop with you. At the highest level, **fulfillment is found in serving something bigger than yourself.** It's the shift from **success to significance.**

Success vs. Significance: The Shift That Changes Everything

At some point in every ambitious woman's journey, a shift happens. You spend years chasing success—the promotions, the business growth, the financial freedom. And when you finally reach a level you once dreamed about, something unexpected happens.

You realize it's not enough.

Not because success isn't meaningful—but because true fulfillment doesn't come from what you accumulate. It comes from what you give.

The highest level of fulfillment is found in service.

It's found in using your skills, resources, and influence to impact something bigger than yourself. It's about moving from success to significance—shifting your focus from what you can achieve to how you can leave a lasting imprint on the world.

That's why service is the ultimate shift.

Because when your success becomes a tool for impact, that's when it truly means something. This is where real joy, purpose, and legacy are built.

What Happens When You Shift from "Me" to "We"

When you stop focusing only on your own fulfillment and start thinking about **who else you can lift up, everything changes.**

Your vision expands. You no longer measure success just by what you accomplish, but by the lives you touch.

You feel deeper purpose. Your work is no longer just about income—it's about impact.

You build something that lasts. Your legacy isn't just a career or a bank account—it's the people you've helped along the way.

The world doesn't need more women who are just *successful*. The world needs more women who are **fulfilled, purpose-driven, and using their success as a force for good.**

Building Your Legacy Through Service

So what happens when you take everything you've built—your knowledge, resources, influence—and use it to serve something bigger?

Because at the end of your life, you won't be remembered just for what you accomplished. You'll be remembered for who you helped, who you lifted, and who you loved through your impact. That is true fulfillment.

And that's the shift that changes everything.

Why Service Is the Key to Lasting Fulfillment

You already know that **success alone doesn't satisfy the soul.** The most fulfilled people aren't the ones who just climb the highest—they are the ones who **lift others as they rise.** When you give—whether it's your time, knowledge, or resources—several things happen:

- You create a legacy that outlives you. Your impact extends far beyond your own career or business.
- You redefine success on your terms. Instead of chasing external validation, you focus on what truly matters.
- **You experience deeper joy and fulfillment.** Contribution brings a sense of purpose that no paycheck ever could.

The Power of Service in Action: Two Women Who Changed the World

The world's most impactful women didn't just build empires—they **used their success as a platform for service.**

Here are two powerhouse women who led through service and **left a legacy far beyond their careers.**

1. Oprah Winfrey: Using Influence to Educate and Empower

Oprah Winfrey is one of the most recognizable and successful women in the world. She built an empire as a media mogul, becoming the first Black female billionaire.

But Oprah's true impact isn't just in television or business. It's in **how she has used her success to serve and uplift others.**

- She established The Oprah Winfrey Leadership Academy for Girls in South Africa, providing education to underprivileged young women who would otherwise have little opportunity to succeed.
- She has donated over $400 million to educational causes, scholarships, and mentorship programs.
- Her Angel Network has built schools, homes, and provided relief efforts in over 30 countries.

Her philosophy? **"To whom much is given, much is required."**

She didn't just build wealth—she used it as a tool to transform lives.

Lesson from Oprah: If you have **resources, influence, or knowledge,** don't hoard them—use them to open doors for others.

2. Sara Blakely: Turning Business Success into Women's Empowerment

Sara Blakely, the founder of Spanx, didn't just revolutionize shapewear—she redefined what's possible for female entrepreneurs.

When she became a billionaire, she made a decision: **She wasn't going to just enjoy her wealth—she was going to invest in other women.**

- She committed to giving away half her wealth to charity through the Giving Pledge.
- She launched the Red Backpack Fund, donating $5 million to support women-owned businesses struggling during COVID-19.
- She consistently funds female entrepreneurs, mentorship programs, and initiatives that level the playing field for women in business.

Her success wasn't just about her—it was about creating opportunities for other women to succeed.

Lesson from Sara: Success means little if you're the only one winning. **Lift others up as you rise.**

How to Integrate Service into Your Life (Without Burnout)

As a powerhouse, your time is valuable. You might be thinking: *"I want to serve, but I'm already stretched thin."* Here's the secret: **Service doesn't have to mean sacrificing yourself.** It simply means **being intentional about how you contribute.**

1. Start with Your Strengths

Instead of forcing yourself into service that doesn't align with you, ask:

- What am I naturally good at that could help others?
- What knowledge or skills do I have that could create impact?
- What cause deeply resonates with me?

If you're an incredible connector, mentor younger women.

If you're a strategic thinker, help a nonprofit streamline its operations.

If you're financially blessed, fund scholarships or women-owned businesses.

Service should feel energizing, not exhausting.

2. Think Bigger Than Charity—Think Legacy

Giving money is great, but true impact is about creating something that lasts.

Instead of just donating, think:

- How can I build something that continues to serve after I'm gone?
- How can I create opportunities that empower others to build their own success?

Legacy isn't just about what you give—it's about what you create that keeps giving.

3. Make Service a Non-Negotiable Part of Success

The most successful women don't wait until they "have more time" to give back.

They build it into their routine.

- Join a board of a cause you care about.
- Mentor one woman a year.
- Host an annual event that supports your community.
- Launch a foundation or fund that aligns with your values.

Service isn't an afterthought—it's a pillar of a fulfilled life.

True fulfillment includes contribution. When you use your voice, gifts, wisdom, and presence to bless others, you don't just make a difference—you experience a deeper kind of joy. Service connects your life to something greater.

The Ripple Effect: When You Give, You Receive More Than You Ever Expected.

One of the greatest myths about success is that it's a solo journey.

In reality, **the more you give, the more you receive.**

- When you mentor, you grow as a leader.
- When you invest in others, you build stronger relationships.
- When you serve, you deepen your own fulfillment.

Because real wealth isn't measured in money alone—it's measured in the lives you impact.

What Will Your Legacy Be?

At the end of your life, what do you want to be remembered for?

Will it be the titles you earned? The money you made? The deals you closed?

Or will it be the lives you touched, the impact you created, and the doors you opened for others?

Success is about you. Significance is about others.

If you want true fulfillment, don't just chase personal wins. **Use your success as a tool to serve something bigger than yourself.**

That's where real legacy is built.

YOUR ACTION PLAN: Creating Impact Now

- **Define Your Cause**—What issue, group, or initiative are you passionate about?
- **Identify Your Strengths**—How can you serve in a way that aligns with your skills?
- **Start Small, Scale Big**—Don't wait until "one day." Start now and build over time.
- **Commit to Consistency**—Make service a part of your life, not just a one-time effort.

Because **your success matters—but what you do with it matters even more.**

What's Next?

You now hold the blueprint for a fulfilled life. In Part 1, we explored the foundational elements—identity, energy, faith, love, meaningful work, and growth. These aren't just lofty ideals; they are the core pillars that shape how you experience your life, relationships, and purpose. But knowledge alone doesn't change us—implementation does. Insight becomes transformation when it meets aligned action.

That's where we go next. Part 2 is about building your roadmap—putting structure to your intentions and momentum behind your vision. Here, we'll take the work you've already done and bring it to life in your daily rhythms, decision-making, and long-term goals. It's time to stop waiting for the "right time" and start living what you now know to be true. This is where fulfillment gets real. Let's begin.

PART 2:
Implementation

CHAPTER 7
Building The Life Of Your Dreams
Creating Your Roadmap

"Create the highest, grandest vision possible for your life, because you become what you believe."
– Oprah Winfrey

Throughout my life, I've regularly heard personal development experts and "gurus" talk about setting five- or ten-year goals. While long-term visioning is helpful, it can sometimes feel too abstract—like a "someday" plan rather than a roadmap for action. Instead, I've found that focusing on a **three-year vision** with a detailed one-year roadmap makes goal setting more tangible and actionable. In fact, most high-achieving women I know who set three-to-five year targets often find themselves hitting those "long-term" goals in six to twelve months. Life is simply too fast-paced to really imagine what's truly possible in 10 years. The realistic 10-year goals likely feel like a pipedream right now, while three years is concrete and tangible.

With that in mind, this chapter will walk you step by step through the process of **mapping your path forward**, breaking big goals into achievable milestones, and designing daily and weekly habits that support long-term success. By the end of this chapter, you'll have a concrete action plan that aligns with your goals, priorities, and the life you want to create.

Step 1: Life Alignment Check-In

On a scale of 1 to 10, rate your current level of *satisfaction* in each of the following areas of your life:

1–2 = Deeply Dissatisfied / In Crisis

This area feels neglected or painful. It's causing stress or harm and needs urgent attention or change.

3–4 = Disconnected / Struggling

There's some awareness of what's not working, but you're not sure how to fix it. This area feels frustrating or heavy.

5 = Neutral / Tolerating

This area is "fine" on the surface but lacks joy, energy, or intentionality. You're going through the motions or settling for less than you desire—but it's not actively painful. You know there's room for improvement, but it hasn't been a top priority.

6-7 = Somewhat Aligned / Improving

This area is working in some ways, but not consistently. You've made progress, but there's still work to do to get where you want to be. It feels hopeful but incomplete.

8-9 = Aligned & Energizing

You feel proud of this area and how you show up in it. It feels mostly aligned with your values, and it brings you energy, peace, or satisfaction.

10 = Fully Aligned / Thriving

This area feels deeply fulfilling, joyful, and fully aligned with who you are. It exemplifies what's possible when you live with intention and integrity.

Health & Fitness

(Vitality, Strength, Resilience, Energy)

- Mental
- Emotional

Self-Love

- Confidence
- Sense of Identity
- Authenticity
- Respect
- Dignity
- Care
- Integrity

Relationships (Connection, Love, Support, Belonging, Loyalty)

- Family
- Friends

- Partner/Spouse
- Children

Overall Well-being

- Peace
- Joy
- Rest
- Harmony

Career

- Impact
- Contribution
- Freedom & Flexibility
- Creativity & Innovation
- Leadership
- Service

Money & Finances

- Wealth / Financial Freedom
- Stability
- Generosity

Spiritual Life

- Connection with God/Spirit
- Faith
- Purpose
- Gratitude

Fun, Recreation

- Play
- Pleasure in Daily Life
- Beauty

- Presence
- Adventure

Personal Growth

- Learning
- Challenge
- Achievement
- Influence
- Curiosity

Life Alignment Reflection

1. Where are you settling in life? What are you tolerating that you don't want to accept anymore? What have you been avoiding or deprioritizing?
2. Which areas do you feel are most in alignment with what you want?
3. Which areas have the most significant gap between where you are and where you want to be? What would a "10" look and feel like in those areas?
4. What's one area where you want massive transformation? Describe what full alignment would look like for you—without limitations or compromise. What would need to shift?
5. If you could shift just one habit, boundary, or belief in one of your lowest-rated categories, what would move the needle most?

Step 2: Clarify Your Vision

Before you can build a roadmap, you need to know where you're going. Start by thinking about your ideal life **three years from now**.

Visualization Exercise

> Access the *audio* version of this visualization at www.LimitlessBookResources.com.

Visualize your life in three years. Ask yourself:

What does your **health** look like?

- How do you *feel* in your body each day—energized, clear-headed, strong, rested?
- What types of movement or exercise are part of your lifestyle? Are you lifting weights, doing yoga, hiking, or dancing?
- What is your relationship with food—do you feel nourished, in control, and aligned with your goals?
- What are your energy levels like throughout the day? Are you alert, present, and calm—even during stressful moments?
- Have you overcome any chronic symptoms or conditions—like fatigue, insulin resistance, anxiety, pain?
- What do your labs or health metrics say—are you metabolically healthy, hormonally balanced, and inflammation-free?
- What do you no longer tolerate regarding your health—poor habits, self-neglect, overcommitting, numbing out?
- What does your self-talk sound like—do you encourage yourself, celebrate progress, and show grace when things don't go as planned?
- Who supports your health—do you have a coach, functional medicine doctor, accountability partner, or a community around you?
- What does self-care look like for you—and how have you finally given yourself permission to prioritize it?

What do your **relationships** feel like?

- How do you feel when you walk into a room with your closest people—seen, supported, energized, at peace?
- Are your relationships life-giving or draining? Do you feel safe to be your full self with the people closest to you?
- How is your connection with your partner or spouse—are you communicating openly, having fun together, growing together, and prioritizing intimacy (emotional and physical)?
- What does your relationship with your children look like—are you present, attuned, and creating memories together? Do you feel confident and proud of how you're showing up as a parent?
- Who are your closest friends—and how often do you connect? Do these friendships challenge and support you? Do they reflect the future you're building?
- Are you setting and holding boundaries in relationships that used to leave you depleted or resentful?
- Have you released or redefined relationships that were no longer aligned with who you're becoming?
- How are you showing up differently in your relationships—more vulnerable, honest, loving, patient, or bold?
- What kinds of conversations are you having regularly—surface-level or deep and growth-oriented?

Are you part of a **community** that truly gets you? Where you can give and receive support without pressure or performance?

- Do you have a place where you can show up fully—without needing to prove, impress, or pretend?
- How do you feel when you're with this community—energized, accepted, inspired, grounded?

- Are you surrounded by people who share your values, vision, or hunger for growth?
- Do you feel emotionally safe to speak your truth, share your struggles, and celebrate your wins without shrinking or apologizing?
- Are you able to ask for help without guilt? Do you genuinely enjoy offering support to others without feeling used or drained?
- How often are you connecting with this group—weekly calls, monthly meetups, group texts, retreats? What does that rhythm look like?
- What types of conversations are happening? Are you talking about real life, real dreams, and real challenges?
- Do you leave those conversations feeling more like yourself—not less?
- Are you cultivating relationships where you're not the only giver or achiever? Where mutual growth and encouragement are the norm?
- How is this community helping you expand your identity, stretch your vision, or stay aligned with your purpose?
- Is this the kind of community you once dreamed about but never believed you'd find?
- What did it take to find or build this community—did you step out of your comfort zone, invest in a program, start your own circle, or say yes to the right room?
- Have you repaired any relationships that needed healing—or have you found peace with letting go?
- What legacy are you creating in your relationships—what would your children or loved ones say about how you made them feel?

What kind of **work** are you doing?

- What excites you when you wake up in the morning—what kind of work are you doing that energizes rather than exhausts you?
- Are you building something of your own, leading a team, consulting, creating, mentoring, writing, and speaking?
- How does your work align with your values and the impact you want to make in the world?
- Are you working for a company that recognizes your gifts—or have you stepped into entrepreneurship, using your talents to build something that reflects your vision?
- How much flexibility and freedom do you have in your schedule? Are you working from home, traveling, or setting your own hours?
- What does your calendar look like? Are your days full of meetings and obligations, or do you have space for strategy, creativity, and rest?
- Who are you working with—are they people who inspire you, challenge you, and treat you with respect?
- Are you doing work that matters to you—or that matters to others? Ideally, both.
- What problems are you solving? What kind of results are you delivering? Are you known for your excellence, perspective, and ability to move people or businesses forward?
- Are you being paid well—not just fairly, but abundantly—for the value you bring?
- How does your work contribute to your sense of fulfillment, purpose, and legacy?
- What are you no longer doing—work that drains you, clients who undervalue you, projects that feel like a mismatch?
- Have you released the need to hustle for your worth and instead stepped into a flow of aligned contribution?

What level of **financial freedom** have you achieved?

- How does it *feel* to make decisions—are they driven by alignment, not anxiety? Do you feel calm and confident when you think about money?
- Do you have consistent income streams that match your lifestyle and values? Are you earning in an aligned, ethical, and expansive way?
- Are your bills, savings, and investments handled with ease—not stress?
- Have you built margin—financial space that allows you to say yes to opportunities and no to what no longer serves you?
- Can you take time off, go on vacation, or say yes to an experience without first checking your bank account or feeling guilty?
- How much money are you earning—and how much are you keeping, investing, or giving away?
- Have you paid off debts that once weighed you down? Are you living with a sense of peace, knowing you're not just surviving but thriving?
- Do you have an emergency fund, long-term investments, and possibly generational wealth in the making?
- Are you building assets—properties, businesses, intellectual property, investments—that grow without trading hours for dollars?
- What does financial independence look like for you—is it about retiring early, funding a dream, supporting your kids, or giving generously?
- How has your financial freedom impacted your relationships, energy, and ability to give back or serve more deeply?

- Are you working from a place of desire rather than desperation—choosing projects because you *want* to, not because you *have* to?
- What beliefs or habits have you shifted to create this freedom? Are you more educated, empowered, and confident with money than ever before?

What does your **daily life** look like?

- How do you start your morning?
- What time do you wake up?
- What is your morning routine like, and how does it support your well-being?
- When do you start work?
- When do you finish work?
- Are you working in an office or from home?
- Can you work from anywhere?
- Do you travel for work?
- Who makes dinner?
- Who cleans up and puts the kids to bed?
- When do you put your phone away?
- What is your evening routine like?
- What time do you go to bed?
- How is your sleep? Do you fall asleep easily and wake up refreshed?

What **experiences** are you enjoying?

- How are you spending your free time—and are you making space for joy, adventure, and rest?
- What trips or vacations are you taking—are you exploring new cities, relaxing by the ocean, hiking mountains, or going on spontaneous weekend getaways?

- What memories are you creating with your family—game nights, road trips, beach days, traditions that light you all up?
- Are you celebrating your milestones—launches, birthdays, anniversaries, goals met—with intention and joy?
- What new things have you tried—dancing lessons, learning a language, hosting dinner parties, starting a podcast, writing a book?
- Are you experiencing beauty regularly—sunsets, art, music, nature, good food, deep conversation?
- What types of self-care do you no longer delay—spa days, quiet mornings, spiritual retreats, long walks with your thoughts?
- Are you enjoying luxury in your own way—flying first class, upgrading your hotel room, eating at your favorite restaurants without guilt, investing in high-quality clothes or skincare?
- What traditions or rituals have you created that fill your soul?
- Are you attending live events—concerts, conferences, retreats—that connect you with others and expand your perspective?
- Do you have space for spontaneity, or are you still over-scheduled and overcommitted?
- What are you doing simply because it makes you feel *alive*—not because it's productive, expected, or required?
- How do you **feel** in your body, mind, and spirit?

In Your Body

- Do you feel strong, energized, and confident in your physical body?

- Are you free of pain, inflammation, or chronic fatigue that once held you back?
- Do you move daily—because it feels good, not because you're punishing yourself?
- What do your clothes feel like on your body—do you feel powerful, sexy, comfortable, radiant?
- Are you nourishing yourself well—hydrating, fueling, and honoring your body with love instead of shame?
- Do you feel connected to your body—tuned into its signals and able to respond with compassion?

In Your Mind

- Is your mental space calm, focused, and clear?
- Have you quieted the self-doubt and anxiety that used to run on a loop in the background?
- Are you practicing mindfulness, presence, and thought leadership in how you speak to yourself and others?
- Do you feel mentally resilient—able to handle challenges without spiraling?
- Are you feeding your mind with inspiration, knowledge, and truth that expands your perspective?
- Have you established routines or habits that protect your peace and sharpen your thinking?

In Your Spirit

- Do you feel deeply connected to something greater than yourself—God, purpose, divine timing?
- Is your inner world anchored in faith, joy, and trust—regardless of circumstances?
- Are you practicing rituals or spiritual habits that restore you—like prayer, meditation, gratitude, or reflection?
- Do you feel aligned with your calling, knowing you're living from your soul and not just your schedule?

- Are you forgiving yourself more easily, releasing shame, and walking in grace?
- Do you feel whole—not because life is flawless, but because you've come home to yourself?

Now that you've visualized the future version of your life—your health, relationships, community, work, finances, experiences, and how you feel in your body, mind, and spirit—**take a moment to let it all sink in.**

This isn't just a daydream. It's a glimpse into what's possible when you choose alignment over obligation, intention over autopilot, and courage over comfort. You don't need to have it all figured out—you just need to be honest about what you *really* want.

Before you move on, pause and put it into words. **Use the following section to describe your life three years from now in vivid, specific detail.** Write as if it's already happening. Speak to the feelings, the freedom, the fulfillment.

Let this be your vision—anchored in truth, guided by desire, and fueled by possibility.

Write Your Three-Year Vision

Imagine it's three years from today, and you're living a deeply aligned, energized, and fulfilling life. Describe that life in vivid detail. Where are you? What does a day in your life look like? How do you feel in your body, mind, and spirit? What kind of work are you doing? Who are you surrounded by? How do you spend your time? What goals have you achieved—and what kind of person have you become?

Write your vision in the present tense as if it's already real. Be bold. Be honest. Let this be a declaration of what's possible.

This is your north star—your long-term vision that will guide your actions.

Step 3: Identify Your Core Goals

Now that you have a vision, it's time to turn it into **specific, actionable goals**.

Write Your Annual Goals

Now, based on your vision, list 10 specific goals for the next year.

For example:

- Become debt-free.
- Take a dream vacation.
- Lose 20 lbs. and build strength.
- Write my book.
- Increase my income by $X.
- Prioritize self-care (weekly spa day, sauna, or personal retreat).

Step 4: Break Your Goals into Milestones

Big goals can feel overwhelming unless they are broken down into smaller, achievable steps.

The Breakdown Process

First Half vs. Second Half of the Year:

- Which goals need to happen in January–June?
- Which goals can you tackle from July–December?

Quarterly Goals (90-day focus): What specific progress should you make each quarter?

Q1:

Q2:

Q3:

Q4:

Monthly Goals:

Each quarter, break your **quarterly goals** into monthly actions.

Month 1:

Month 2:

Month 3:

Weekly Actions:

- Keep a Weekly Planner/Journal.
- What three to five actions will move the needle THIS week?

Step 5: Create Daily & Weekly Habits

Success isn't about big leaps—it's about **small, consistent habits** that compound over time.

Ultimately, fulfillment comes down to how you structure your days—making time for what matters most and ensuring your daily actions reflect your highest priorities.

Questions to Ask Yourself:

What **daily habits** will help you get closer to your goals? (e.g., morning journaling, meal prepping, exercise)

What **weekly habits** will keep you on track? (e.g., setting intentions on Sunday, reviewing progress)

How can you **track** these habits? (e.g., a journal or habit tracker)

Build Your Habit System

Daily Intentions: Write down your top three to five daily priorities.

Weekly Reflection: Every Sunday, review your progress. How did you do?

Monthly Check-ins: Are your goals still aligned with what you want?

Use a Habit Tracker: Download a habit-tracking app, or use a journal to measure success.

Step 6: Identify Challenges & Plan for Setbacks

No journey is smooth—there will be obstacles. Instead of waiting for them to surprise you, **anticipate and plan for them**.

What Might Get in Your Way?

Lack of time? → Schedule time blocking.

Lack of energy? → Prioritize sleep, exercise, and stress management.

Fear or self-doubt? → Find accountability partners and support systems.

Unexpected setbacks? → Have a flexible mindset and contingency plans.

Step 7: Build a Support System

You don't have to do this alone. **Who can help you?**

Household Support: Can your partner or family help with household chores, meal planning, or childcare?

Outsourcing: Can you hire a cleaner, use grocery delivery, or automate tasks?

Mentors & Coaches: Who can provide guidance and accountability?

Community: Join groups or masterminds to stay motivated.

Step 8: Hold Yourself Accountable

The key to long-term success is **consistent accountability**.

Ways to Stay Accountable:

Journaling & Tracking: Keep a daily/weekly log of progress.

Accountability Partners: Check in with a friend, mentor, or coach.

Review Progress Monthly: Adjust goals as needed.

Celebrate Wins: Recognize small successes along the way.

Step 9: Complete Mid-Year and Year-End Goal Reviews

I recommend revisiting your goals and roadmap twice per year. Every July I complete a Mid-year review to assess what's working versus what needs to shift, and whether my goals are still aligned with my vision. I often find that my focus shifts throughout the year so the mid-year review allows me to pivot without guilt.

- Have a goal you're no longer excited about? → Cross it off the list.
- Has a new opportunity presented itself? → Add it to your roadmap and build an action plan.

You make the rules! You can't screw this up. This is your vision and your future.

At year-end, I always do a more comprehensive reflection, asking deeper questions and auditing how I spent my time so I can realign before the next cycle begins.

Recommended Structure for the Ongoing Planning & Review Cycle

1. **Annual Planning** (January or your personal "new year")
   - Use the Roadmap Template and Annual Goal Mapping Worksheets
   - Break down goals into halves (H1, H2), quarters, and months
   - Set aligned habits and accountability structures
2. **Midyear Review (July)**
   - Revisit your Roadmap and reassess goals
   - Reflect on what's working, what's changed, and what needs to be released or recalibrated
3. **Year-End Review (December)**
   - Reflect deeply on the past year
   - Celebrate wins, examine challenges, and do a Calendar Audit
   - Use your insights to inform your next Annual Planning Cycle

The nine steps in this chapter offer a powerful framework for building a life that honors your values and brings your three-year vision to life. They allow you to implement a rhythm so your roadmap becomes a living, breathing part of how you lead your life.

> For detailed worksheets to further support you in this process download the Fulfilled & Limitless Workbook in the resources page at www.LimitlessBookResources.com.

CHAPTER 8

Building Habits & Routines To Support Your Roadmap

Aligning Your Habits with the Life You're Creating

"Success doesn't come from what you do occasionally. It comes from what you do consistently."
– Marie Forleo

Why Habits and Routines Matter

If you've made it this far in the book, you already know that fulfillment isn't something that magically happens—it's something you create through **consistent, intentional habits** that shape your energy, mindset, and focus.

Your habits are the **invisible force behind everything you do.** They determine whether you wake up feeling energized or exhausted, whether you start your day focused or frazzled, and whether you consistently make progress on what matters most or get caught up in distractions.

Let's get one thing straight—this is not about having a **perfect morning routine** or checking off a long list of rituals just because someone on social media told you that you *have* to. You will never hear me say, "If you don't wake up at 5 AM and drink warm lemon water before journaling and meditating, you're failing at life." No. Life is messy, unpredictable, and full of curveballs. **The key is to create habits and routines that work for you, not against you.**

But here's the truth: If you want to live a fulfilled life, **you must set yourself up for success daily.** Your habits and routines are the structure that allows you to consistently show up as the person you want to be. They help you eliminate decision fatigue, free up mental energy, and ensure that the essentials are covered no matter what happens in your day.

The habits and routines you build now will **determine the trajectory of your life.** The small things you do daily—**not the big, once-a-year efforts—shape your fulfillment, energy, and success.**

Start small. Keep it simple. Make it feel good. **And most importantly, keep it going.**

The Science of Building Better Habits

You don't need more motivation—you need a system.

James Clear explains in his bestselling book *Atomic Habits*, "You do not rise to the level of your goals. You fall to the level of your systems." That means it's not about willpower or intensity—it's about building an environment and a rhythm that makes success inevitable.

Habits are the invisible architecture of our daily lives. The key is to make small, consistent choices that compound over time.

Here's how to make them stick:

1. Stack Your Habits (Attach them to something you already do)

This is called *habit stacking*, and it's one of the most effective ways to embed new behaviors into your life. You simply tie a new habit to something that's already part of your routine.

Examples:

- *If you drink coffee every morning*, use that time to write down three things you're grateful for.
- *If you brush your teeth every night*, take that moment to do a 60-second, deep breathing exercise.
- *If you check your calendar before work*, review your top three priorities for the day at the same time.

Linking your new habit to an existing cue helps your brain recognize when it's time to act—without relying on motivation.

2. Make It Obvious (Create visual or environmental reminders)

According to Clear, one of the most overlooked drivers of behavior is your environment. You're far more likely to follow through on a habit when the reminder is right in front of you.

Examples:

- *If you want to take vitamins*, put them next to your toothbrush or coffee mug.
- *If you want to drink more water*, keep a full bottle on your desk or nightstand.
- *If you want to journal*, leave your notebook on your pillow so you see it before bed.

The goal is to make the habit so visible and frictionless that you can't ignore it.

3. Start Small (Make It ridiculously easy)

One of the biggest reasons we fail to follow through on habits is that we start too big. Clear emphasizes the power of *The Two-Minute Rule*: every habit should be so easy at first, you can't say no.

Examples:

- Don't aim for a 30-minute workout—start with five minutes of movement.
- Don't commit to reading a full chapter—read one page before bed.
- Don't plan to overhaul your diet overnight—start by adding one protein-rich meal per day.

Small wins build momentum. And once you start, it's easier to keep going.

4. Add Pleasure to Your Routines

Your habits shouldn't feel like punishment—they should be something you look forward to. According to Clear, a habit that feels good is more likely to stick. This is especially important for women who are used to white knuckling their way through routines. Sustainability comes from joy, not deprivation.

Ask yourself:

What small pleasures can I pair with my healthy habits?

- Light a candle while journaling?
- Listen to a favorite podcast while walking?
- Use fancy hand cream after brushing my teeth?

The most powerful women I know—the ones who seem to "have it all together"—aren't running on willpower alone. They have **systems** in place. They've made their self-care, energy, and mindset non-negotiable. And it's not because they're lucky or disciplined; it's because they've **made these things automatic** through habits.

Let's get you there too.

What Habits and Routines Do You Actually Need?

Not every habit or routine will work for you—and that's OK. The goal isn't to mimic someone else's ideal schedule. The goal is to **design rhythms that support your energy, priorities, and goals**. For high-performing women, the right habits aren't about doing more—they're about aligning with who you are and who you're becoming.

Start by asking yourself:

- What habits would help me feel more energized every day?

- What habits would help me stay focused and productive?
- What routines would reduce stress and bring me peace?
- What habits would bring me joy and pleasure?
- What habits would help me reach my long-term goals?

Then, take inventory of what you already do naturally. Maybe you make coffee each morning, brush your teeth before bed, or check your calendar at night. These existing rhythms create the scaffolding of your day and are the perfect places to build from.

But more importantly: **What habits do you actually need right now?**

Here are some categories to consider based on your goals and the season you're in:

If you're in a season of growth or expansion:

- Morning journaling or visualization to stay connected to your bigger vision
- Weekly CEO time to strategize and zoom out from the daily grind
- Deep work blocks or time blocking to protect your focus
- Networking or outreach habits that grow your influence and impact

If you're recovering from burnout or managing stress:

- Midday breathwork or short walks to regulate your nervous system
- Strict work shut-down rituals to protect your evenings
- Evening wind-down routines (no screens, calming rituals, earlier bedtime)
- Saying "no" as a habit—learning to pause before overcommitting

If you're juggling family and leadership:

- Early morning quiet time before the house wakes up
- Pre-dinner rituals to transition out of work mode
- Connection habits with your partner or children (like 10-min check-ins)
- Weekend planning sessions to ease the mental load

If you're focused on becoming your next-level self:

- Gratitude or celebration rituals to anchor success and joy
- Weekly reflection to identify what's working (and what's not)
- Regular learning—reading, podcast listening, or courses that challenge your thinking
- Decluttering habits that create spaciousness—physically, mentally, and emotionally

You don't need a dozen new habits. You just need a few **on-purpose** ones—habits that create momentum and reinforce the identity you're building. Choose what matters most, and design rhythms that reflect the life you want to live. And remember: **Your habits should serve you—not the other way around.** Let them be simple. Let them be life-giving. Let them shift as your needs change.

The Power of Bookends—Morning and Evening Routines

As a certified *Heroic Coach* trained under Brian Johnson's *Heroic* methodology, I've seen firsthand the profound impact of what he calls **"bookends"**—your morning and evening routines. According to Brian, while we can't always control the chaos that happens between sunrise and sunset, we *can* take full ownership of how we begin and end each day. And that ownership is where our true power lies.

Your bookends are more than just habits—they are identity-shaping anchors. These moments are when you consciously choose how you want to show up in the world, reinforcing your values, energy, and purpose.

Why Morning and Evening Routines Matter

- **They give you back control.** Even if the middle of your day is unpredictable, your bookends are yours. They're the foundation upon which you build the rest of your day.
- **They train your nervous system.** Morning routines prime your physiology to be focused, energized, and present. Night routines help your body shift into rest, recovery, and restoration. When these transitions are intentional, they reduce stress and increase resilience.
- **They build trust and integrity.** Every time you follow through on your bookend habits, you cast a vote for the person you're becoming. Consistency in these rituals compounds over time into unshakable confidence and alignment.
- **They reinforce your identity.** Are you someone who honors your body, purpose, family, and calling? Your routines are where that identity is practiced—not just dreamed about.

- **They support every area of your life.** From better sleep and sharper thinking to improved relationships and deeper fulfillment, the ripple effects of solid bookends touch everything.

When I follow my morning and evening routines, I'm not just checking boxes—I'm aligning with who I want to be. And that's the invitation for you: design your bookends not based on what you *should* do but on who you *want* to become.

Brian always says, "Your day starts the night before." So let's start with your evening routine or PM bookend. This is your chance to close out the day with intention, calm your nervous system, and prime yourself for deep rest and a strong start tomorrow. The truth is, what you do in the hour or two before bed has a **massive impact** on your energy, sleep quality, mental clarity, and emotional resilience the next day. Let's talk about a few high-impact habits and why they matter.

Top Evening Routine Habits to Consider

1. Digital Sunset (Turn off Your Phone One Hour Before Bed)

Brian Johnson calls this a "Digital Sunset" for good reason. Just like the sun naturally signals to your body that it's time to wind down, a digital sunset is your cue to transition from stimulation to stillness.

What it means:

A digital sunset involves **turning off all screens—phones, tablets, TVs, computers—at least one hour before bed**. That includes saying no to late-night Netflix, doomscrolling on social media, or checking email "one last time." Ideally, you'll also **keep your phone out of the bedroom altogether**, using an alarm clock instead.

Why it matters:

- Screens emit blue light, which suppresses melatonin—the hormone that signals your body it's time to sleep.
- Engaging content (social media, news, shows) stimulates your brain, making it harder to fall asleep and stay asleep.
- Keeping your phone nearby can increase dopamine hits and interruptions—even if you don't touch it, your brain stays on alert.
- Creating space away from screens allows your body to relax naturally, leading to deeper, more restorative sleep, helping you wake up with more clarity, energy, and focus.

Many high performers consider this a game-changer for improving sleep and overall energy. It's one of the simplest yet most overlooked ways to transform your nights—and therefore, your days.

Try this tonight:

- Set a specific time for your digital sunset and treat it like a non-negotiable commitment.
- Charge your phone outside your bedroom (or at least across the room, face down and on Do Not Disturb).
- Replace screen time with something nourishing: reading, journaling, stretching, or connecting with someone you love.

Once you experience how much better you sleep without screens, you'll wonder why you ended your day any other way.

2. Stop Eating at Least Two Hours Before Bed

Late-night snacking might be a comfort habit, but it's working against your body's natural rhythms.

Why it matters:

- Eating close to bedtime spikes insulin and delays melatonin production.
- Your body spends the night digesting food instead of entering deep repair mode.
- You're more likely to experience blood sugar crashes that interrupt your sleep.
- Give your digestive system a break and let your body fully shift into recovery mode while you sleep.

3. Wind Down Your Nervous System

Your brain can't just flip a switch and fall asleep. Create a consistent transition routine that helps your body move from alert to relaxed.

Ideas to try:

- Light stretching or restorative yoga
- Deep breathing exercises or guided meditation
- Journaling or a gratitude practice to process the day
- Reading a physical book (fiction or something uplifting)

4. Set the Tone for Tomorrow

A few minutes of preparation at night can remove friction from your morning.

Ideas to try:

- Lay out your clothes or gym gear.
- Review your calendar or top three priorities for the next day.
- Prep your morning smoothie or breakfast.
- Write down anything lingering on your mind (keep a journal beside your bed for this) so you can clear your mind and sleep easier.

Top Morning Routine Habits to Consider

A strong morning routine doesn't need to be long or elaborate. It just needs to be aligned. The purpose is simple: activate your body, focus your mind, and reconnect with who you want to be *before* the world starts pulling at you. But let's be real—mornings aren't always seamless. Some days, you'll wake up energized and ready to go. Other days, you'll hit snooze, feel behind, or barely get out the door. That's life. The goal isn't perfection—it's support. Especially for women who carry the mental and emotional load at home, mornings often mean getting kids fed, dressed, and out the door while still juggling your own responsibilities. That's why it's essential to carve out even a small window of time *before* your kids are up. Once the day begins, the chaos often follows. But if you get even 10 quiet minutes to yourself first? That's where your grounding, focus, and power begin.

Here are some powerful morning habits to consider:

1. Hydrate First Thing

After seven-eight hours of sleep, your body is dehydrated. Drink 16 ounces of water right when you wake up.

Why it matters:

- Jumpstarts digestion and metabolism
- Supports mental clarity and physical energy
- Helps flush out toxins
- Add a pinch of sea salt or a splash of lemon for extra minerals and electrolyte balance.

2. Get Morning Sunlight

Getting natural light within the first hour of waking helps regulate your circadian rhythm.

Why it matters:

- Boosts mood and alertness
- Supports hormone regulation (like cortisol and melatonin)
- Helps reset your sleep-wake cycle for better energy throughout the day
- Even five-ten minutes outside or near a window can make a difference.

3. Practice Stillness (Prayer, Meditation, or Breathwork)

Before reaching for your phone, ground yourself in peace and presence.

Why it matters:

- Activates the parasympathetic nervous system
- Lowers stress and anxiety
- Creates space to connect with your inner wisdom or faith
- Even three-five minutes of quiet can recenter your entire day.

4. Move Your Body

If you can fit in a full 30-minute workout, that's fantastic! But you don't need a complete workout to succeed in this—just move your body.

Options:

- Stretching, yoga, or foam rolling
- A brisk walk
- A strength or cardio session

Why it matters:

- Boosts energy and blood flow

- Enhances mental clarity and motivation
- Increases dopamine and endorphins

5. Set Your Intentions for the Day

Before diving into your to-do list, define what truly matters.

Try this:

Write down your top one–three priorities.

Reflect on how you want to show up (courageous, present, joyful?)

Visualize the kind of person you want to be today.

This isn't about perfection—it's about alignment.

6. Gratitude Practice

Start your day by noticing what's already good. Write down three to five things you are grateful for each morning.

Why it matters:

- Shifts your focus from lack to abundance
- Boosts happiness and emotional well-being
- Trains your brain to look for the positive

Simple ideas:

- Write down three things you're grateful for.
- Reflect on one thing that brought you joy yesterday.
- Send a quick text of appreciation to someone you care about.

My Evening Routine:

I've designed a **night routine I actually look forward to**—one that helps me transition from a full, productive day to a state of rest.

- Stop eating at least two hours before bed to regulate my blood sugar and give my body time to digest my dinner.
- Take magnesium & my nighttime supplements to help my body unwind.
- Put my kids to bed—baths, books, prayers, and plenty of cuddle time.
- Turn off my phone at least one hour before bed.
- Enjoy my skincare routine—I use high-quality, organic skincare that doesn't fill my body with unnecessary toxins. I breathe in my favorite face oil like I'm at the spa.
- Read or journal to clear my mind before sleep.
- Lay on my PEMF mat and let my body relax.
- Turn out the light and take three deep breaths. For each breath, I breathe in for four seconds through my nose, then out for eight seconds through my mouth.

My Morning Routine:

My morning routine has to be flexible to support my busy life and family. Below is an example of an ideal day, but it often gets cut short when something comes up. During seasons where I can't wake up before my kids do, I rely on my husband and nanny for additional support with the kids.

- Wake up at least one hour before my kids do.
- Lay on my PEMF mat for 10 minutes to ease into the day and support my muscles and circulation.
- Go to the bathroom and brush my teeth.
- If I have extra time, I will stand in front of my red light for 10 minutes. Otherwise, I skip this step.
- Put on my workout clothes.
- Read my Bible and daily devotion. Read, pray, and journal.

- Gratitude Practice: I write down five things I'm grateful for each morning.
- Intentions: I write down three intentions for the day.
- Make and drink my morning smoothie.
- Work Out: I walk outside for 30 minutes or bike on my Peloton. Twice a week, I go to Discover Strength for strength training workouts.
- Shower and get dressed.
- Get everyone ready and out the door as needed.

Exercise: Build Your Evening & Morning Routines

Now it's your turn: Choose five to ten habits for both your evening & morning routines that will set you up for success each day.

Your Evening Routine

1.
2.
3.
4.
5.
6.
7.
8.
9.
10.

Your Morning Routine

1.
2.
3.
4.
5.
6.
7.
8.
9.
10.

Build Routines That Work for YOU

Ultimately, habits and routines aren't about rigid rules or picture-perfect schedules—they're about creating structure that supports the life you want to live. The most fulfilled, high-performing women I know don't rely on willpower alone. They've built rhythms that anchor their energy, protect their peace, and keep them aligned with who they're becoming. Whether it's a digital sunset that leads to deeper sleep, a morning routine that grounds your focus before the chaos begins, or a few small practices that reconnect you to gratitude and purpose—these seemingly simple actions add up to a powerful foundation.

You don't need to overhaul your life or stack your days with endless rituals. You just need a few intentional habits—morning and night—that reinforce the woman you want to be. Start small. Choose what matters. Build in a way that feels both supportive and sustainable. When your habits align with your values, energy, and vision, they become more than just checkboxes. They become the quiet, consistent force behind your fulfillment—and the roadmap you can return to, no matter the season you're in.

CHAPTER 9
Overcoming "Failure" And Setbacks
Turning Setbacks Into Stepping Stones

"Failure is a necessary part of success.
See it as a stepping stone to mastery."
– Christi Cossette

Setbacks are inevitable, but how you respond to them determines your path forward. Too often, we view setbacks as roadblocks rather than redirections. In reality, setbacks often reveal important lessons, clarify our desires, and strengthen our resilience. They challenge us to reflect, adapt, and grow beyond what we initially believed we could achieve.

The Mindset Shift: From Failure to Growth

One of the most powerful changes you can make is to stop seeing setbacks as failures and start seeing them as opportunities for growth. Every challenge you face is a chance to learn something new about yourself, your path, and your goals. It's easy to get frustrated when things don't go as planned, but what if the setback pushes you toward something greater?

For example, I once took on a project that I believed would catapult my career to the next level. I invested significant time, energy, and effort into it, only to have it fall apart due to circumstances beyond my control. At first, I was extremely frustrated. But as I reflected on the experience, I realized how much I had learned—about leadership, resilience, and handling adversity. That so-called failure ended up preparing me for an even bigger opportunity down the road.

Another example is found in the stories of some of the most successful people in the world. Thomas Edison famously said, "I have not failed. I've just found 10,000 ways that won't work." Walt Disney was fired from a newspaper for "lacking imagination." Oprah Winfrey was told she was unfit for television. If they had allowed setbacks to define them, they would never have reached their full potential. Instead, they used them as learning experiences and stepping stones to something greater.

Accepting What You Can't Control

One of the hardest lessons in overcoming setbacks is recognizing what is within your control and what isn't. There are times when, no matter how much effort you put in, things simply don't work out the way you hoped. Learning to accept this reality is freeing—it allows you to focus on what you *can* change and release the burden of what you can't.

Take job loss as an example. Many professionals experience layoffs, not because of their performance but due to budget cuts, restructuring, or external economic factors. If you define yourself by your job, a layoff can feel like a personal failure. However, the truth is that your skills, experience, and worth are not diminished just because a company makes a business decision. What you *can* control is how you respond—whether you use the time to upskill, pivot, or seek out a new opportunity that better aligns with your long-term goals.

I truly believe that everything in my life has happened for me, not to me. I trust that God is guiding me toward something better, even if I can't see it yet. Yes, it can be painful to leave behind relationships and a work environment you love. But growth stops when you stay in your comfort zone. And I refuse to stay stuck.

The same principle applies to relationships. Not all friendships or romantic relationships will last forever, no matter how much effort you put in. People change, circumstances evolve, and sometimes, despite your best intentions, relationships end. Rather than dwelling on what went wrong, it's important to focus on what you learned from the experience and how it can help you in future relationships.

Embracing Life's Seasons

Just as nature transitions through different seasons, so do our lives. Each season of life brings its challenges, rewards, and transitions. Some seasons may feel abundant and full of joy, while others may be marked by hardship and struggle. Understanding that life moves in cycles helps us develop patience and grace for ourselves.

In our careers, we may experience seasons of rapid growth and advancement, followed by slower periods where we feel stagnant. Instead of viewing these slower seasons as failures, consider them opportunities for rest, reflection, and strategic planning for what's next. Similarly, in our personal lives, we may go through seasons of nurturing relationships and family, while at other times, we may need solitude and self-discovery.

When facing a difficult season, it's essential to trust that it will not last forever. Just as winter inevitably gives way to spring, tough times will pass, and new opportunities will emerge. Learning to embrace each season for what it offers—rather than resisting it—allows us to find peace and purpose in every phase of our journey.

To better navigate life's seasons, consider the following strategies:

Recognize the Season You Are In—Understanding whether you are in a period of growth, rest, challenge, or transition can help you respond appropriately.

Adjust Expectations—If you're in a season of struggle, it's OK to slow down. If you're in a season of rapid change, embrace it.

Prepare for Transitions—Just like we prepare for seasonal weather changes, we can prepare for life's transitions by building resilience, seeking knowledge, and maintaining flexibility.

Find Gratitude in Each Season—Even difficult seasons have hidden blessings. Reflecting on what each season teaches you fosters appreciation and growth.

Stay Open to Change—Life rarely follows a straight path. Being open to shifting priorities and new opportunities makes transitions smoother.

Embracing life's cyclical nature allows us to experience growth and fulfillment without unnecessary resistance. Each phase serves a purpose, and the more we learn to flow with life rather than fight against it, the more peace and success we will find.

The Importance of Adaptability: It's OK to Change Your Mind

One of the most underrated strengths in life is adaptability. Shifting direction, reconsidering choices, and embracing change allow for continuous growth. Too often, people feel pressured to stick with decisions simply because they have already invested time, effort, or money into them. However, changing your mind when circumstances change or new insights arise is entirely OK.

When making decisions, it can help to categorize them as *temporary* or *permanent*. Temporary decisions can be adjusted without significant long-term consequences, while permanent decisions require deeper consideration. If you find yourself feeling stuck, ask:

- Is this a long-term commitment, or can I reevaluate it later?
- What is the worst that could happen if I change my mind?
- Am I holding onto this decision because of fear or because it's still the right path for me?

For instance, I once committed to a business partnership that seemed like the perfect opportunity. As months passed, I realized that it was not aligned with my vision, and I struggled with backing out. The turning point came when I accepted that changing course was not a failure, but an act of self-awareness and realignment.

Permitting yourself to pivot allows you to make decisions with confidence, knowing that if circumstances change, you have the power to adjust. Adaptability is not about being indecisive; it is about being wise enough to recognize when a new direction is necessary.

Moving Forward with Confidence

Overcoming setbacks is not about avoiding challenges but about learning how to navigate them with resilience. You build strength and character each time you push through a difficult moment. Remember, your journey is unfolding exactly as it should. Trust that what lies ahead is even greater than what you've left behind.

So the next time you encounter a setback, take a deep breath, remind yourself of your strength, and keep moving forward. You are capable, you are resilient, and you are on the right path.

CHAPTER 10
Overcoming Roadblocks

The Hidden Barriers Keeping You Stuck

"You can't reach your next level if you're not willing to face what's standing in your way. Identifying and overcoming your roadblocks is non-negotiable."
– Christi Cossette

What happens when you've done all the "right" things—you've built your career, put in the work, checked all the success boxes—and yet, something still feels *off*? You know you're capable of more, but no matter how hard you push, something keeps getting in the way.

If this sounds familiar, you're not alone. Female executives and high-achieving women face a **unique set of roadblocks** on the path to fulfillment. And most of the time, they aren't external. They aren't about the lack of opportunity or skills. They're **internal barriers**—deeply ingrained beliefs, patterns, and fears that keep us from stepping fully into our potential.

Why We Stay Stuck

Let me be clear: It's **not** about being good enough. You're more than capable. If you weren't, you wouldn't have made it this far. But success doesn't mean fulfillment. And just because you *can* do it all doesn't mean you *should*. Many of the roadblocks we face aren't obvious. They aren't things you can just "push through" with sheer willpower. They require a different kind of work that forces you to **look inward** and ask the tough questions.

So let's do that.

In this chapter, we're breaking down the **most common roadblocks that keep female executives from truly fulfilling and achieving their biggest dreams**—and more importantly, how to move past them.

Roadblock #1: The Need for External Validation

As high-achieving women, we've spent much of our lives proving ourselves to others. Whether it's earning a promotion, securing a prestigious title, or gaining recognition for our accomplishments, the need for external validation has been a powerful motivator.

Society often measures success by tangible markers like salary increases, awards, or recognition from others, and it's easy to fall into the trap of seeking approval from the outside world. However, when your sense of self-worth becomes tied to external recognition, it becomes a roadblock. You start seeking validation in everything you do, which can prevent you from pursuing your true desires, taking risks, and feeling confident in your achievements.

How This Gets in the Way:

The need for external validation can hinder your progress and fulfillment in several ways:

- **Dependency on Praise:** Your sense of accomplishment is only validated when others notice. Without external recognition, you may feel like your efforts are worthless, even if you're achieving great things.
- **Insecurity in Decision-Making:** When seeking approval from others becomes your primary driver, you may avoid making bold career moves or taking risks, fearing disapproval or criticism from peers or superiors.
- **Chronic Overworking:** To maintain a sense of worth, you may constantly push yourself to do more, even when you're physically and mentally drained. You may feel that you're not valuable if you're not continually producing.
- **Lack of Fulfillment:** The more you rely on outside recognition, the less you feel a sense of internal fulfillment. Your happiness and success become conditional on others' perspectives, making it difficult to experience true contentment.
- **Imposter Syndrome:** Even if you achieve something noteworthy, the need for validation can lead to feelings of inadequacy or the belief that you don't truly deserve your accomplishments.

How to Identify It:

- **Unease without Praise:** You feel anxious or deflated when you aren't getting recognition for your work, even if it is meaningful.
- **Fear of Judgment:** You hesitate to make career decisions or pursue opportunities because you fear how others will judge or perceive you, especially if they don't align with traditional notions of success.
- **Inability to Celebrate Yourself:** You feel the need for external acknowledgment before you can truly take pride in your achievements. You struggle to feel proud of yourself until others recognize your success.
- **Constant Hustle:** You're caught in a cycle of doing more and more to earn the validation you crave. Slowing down or taking time for yourself feels like you're failing.
- **People-Pleasing Tendencies:** You prioritize others' needs or approval over your desires and goals, often at the expense of your happiness and well-being.

Ways to Overcome It:

1. **Redefine Success on Your Terms:** Take a step back and reflect on what success means to you. What would you define as a successful life if you stripped away the titles, salary increases, and awards? Understand that success isn't defined by external markers but by the fulfillment you find in your work, growth, and relationships. Create a personalized vision of success that aligns with your values and passions.
2. **Celebrate Your Wins Privately:** Shift your focus from seeking external recognition to acknowledging your achievements on your own. Start writing down three things you're proud of every day, no matter how small they may

seem. This helps build your confidence from within and reinforces the idea that your worth isn't dependent on others' praise.

3. **Detach Your Worth from Productivity:** It's essential to recognize that your value as a person isn't tied to what you do or how much you accomplish. Embrace the understanding that you are valuable simply because you exist, not because of your productivity. Take time to rest, recharge, and focus on nurturing yourself, knowing that slowing down doesn't diminish your worth.

4. **Develop Internal Validation Practices:** Work on validating yourself internally by cultivating self-compassion and self-acceptance. Every time you make a decision or accomplish something, practice acknowledging it to yourself. Trust that your own approval is enough and that you don't need others to confirm your success.

5. **Set Boundaries Around Others' Expectations:** Establish healthy boundaries with those who expect too much from you or may feed into your need for external validation. While feedback and support from others can be valuable, protecting yourself from people or environments that reinforce your dependency on external recognition is important.

6. **Shift from Perfectionism to Progress:** Let go of the pressure to be perfect or constantly perform at your highest level. Embrace the idea that progress, not perfection, is what truly matters. Every step forward, no matter how small, is an achievement worth celebrating.

7. **Engage in Mindfulness and Self-Reflection:** Practice mindfulness to help you stay grounded in the present moment and tune into your inner desires and feelings. Reflect regularly on your accomplishments and growth,

separate from the opinions of others. This helps you cultivate a deeper understanding of your true worth.

The need for external validation is a common roadblock for high-achieving women, especially those who have spent their lives proving themselves to others. While seeking acknowledgment is natural, it's crucial to understand that true fulfillment comes from within. When you can detach your worth from external recognition and redefine success on your own terms, you'll unlock your full potential. You'll be able to confidently pursue your dreams, make decisions without fear of judgment, and experience the satisfaction of knowing that your value doesn't depend on what others think.

Roadblock #2: Fear of Other People's Opinions

The fear of other people's opinions is a deep-seated concern about how others perceive you, often leading to self-doubt and a reluctance to take action. This roadblock can stem from the desire for approval, acceptance, or avoiding judgment. Whether in your personal life, career, or business, the fear of what others might think can prevent you from fully stepping into your potential. You may hesitate to speak your truth, make bold decisions, or pursue dreams because you're overly concerned with how others will interpret your actions.

How This Gets in the Way:
- The fear of others' opinions can hold you back from achieving your true potential in several ways:
- **Self-Sabotage:** You may delay or avoid pursuing opportunities because of fear of judgment. This results in missed chances and unfulfilled goals.
- **Inauthenticity:** The constant need for approval can cause you to suppress your true self, adopting personas that

aren't aligned with your values and aspirations. This leaves you feeling disconnected from your authentic path.
- **Indecision:** Fear of others' reactions can lead to second-guessing decisions and hesitation. This causes delays in moving forward and missed opportunities.
- **Imposter Syndrome:** Constantly comparing yourself to others can make you feel inadequate despite being capable of achieving great things.

How to Identify It:

- **Procrastination due to fear of judgment:** You keep putting off important decisions or projects, thinking you need to wait for the right moment or more approval from others.
- **People-Pleasing:** You prioritize others' needs and opinions over your own, saying "yes" when you want to say "no" and conforming to others' expectations.
- **Overthinking decisions:** You spend excessive time weighing how others will perceive every action you take, causing paralysis by analysis.
- **Seeking external validation:** You often look to others for reassurance before taking any significant steps, relying on their opinions for self-worth or affirmation.
- **Feeling defensive or insecure:** If you feel defensive or overly sensitive to any criticism, it could be a sign that you're too concerned with how others view you.

Ways to Overcome It:

1. **Shift your focus to your values and vision:** Start by identifying what matters most. What are your personal goals and values? When you make decisions based on your values, you free yourself from the influence of others' opinions. Focus on the outcome you desire rather than the judgments of those around you.

2. **Embrace vulnerability and authenticity:** Allow yourself to be real and unapologetically you. The more you embrace your true self, the more you'll attract those who genuinely support and resonate with you rather than seeking validation from those who might not understand your journey.
3. **Reframe criticism as feedback:** Understand that not everyone will agree with you, and that's OK. Reframe negative feedback as an opportunity to grow rather than something that defines your worth. Not all opinions are valuable; you don't need to internalize them.
4. **Take action regardless of others' opinions:** The best way to push through the fear is by taking bold action. Make decisions that align with your goals, and take steps toward them, even if others may not approve. The more you take action, the more you prove to yourself that you don't need others' approval to succeed.
5. **Surround yourself with supportive people:** Build a circle of people who encourage and believe in you. Having a supportive community can help reduce the impact of negative opinions and boost your confidence.
6. **Develop a strong sense of self-worth:** Spend time cultivating self-love and confidence. The more you value yourself and trust in your abilities, the less you'll be affected by external judgments. Focus on what you bring to the table, and remind yourself of your unique strengths.
7. **Practice gratitude and self-affirmation:** Take time each day to affirm your accomplishments, growth, and what you're grateful for. This helps build an internal foundation of worth and reduces the impact of external criticism.
8. **Learn to say no:** Saying no is a powerful way to assert your boundaries and protect your energy. People will respect

you more when you're confident in your decisions, even if they don't always agree with you.

The fear of others' opinions is a silent thief of your potential. It makes you play small, settle for less, and avoid risks that could lead to great rewards. You can reclaim your power by recognizing this fear and confronting it head-on. The key is to prioritize your growth, trust your instincts, and take the necessary steps to live the life you envision, not the life others think you should live. You are worthy of pursuing your dreams, regardless of the opinions of others, and the world needs you to show up as your authentic self.

Roadblock #3: Fear of Being "Too Much"

As women, we've often been told, directly or indirectly, to shrink ourselves, to make ourselves smaller so that we're more "acceptable" to those around us. We've been conditioned to believe that being too ambitious, outspoken, or driven makes us intimidating or unlikable. There's a societal expectation for women to be "nice," "pleasing," and "agreeable," but when we embrace our full power, we are often met with resistance or criticism. This fear of being "too much" causes us to hold back, soften our words, or even shrink into the background, all in an attempt to make others feel more comfortable. We begin to question our brilliance and downplay our accomplishments, afraid of standing out too much. However, when we hold back, we deny ourselves the ability to fully step into the impact we are capable of making.

How This Gets in the Way:

The fear of being "too much" holds us back in several significant ways:

- **Underestimating Your Potential:** When you shrink yourself, you limit your ability to reach your full potential.

By not showing up fully, you miss opportunities to contribute at your highest level and make the impact you're capable of.
- **Lack of Authenticity:** The more you filter yourself or hold back, the further you stray from who you really are. This creates an internal disconnect, making genuine connections and fulfillment from your work and relationships harder.
- **Fear of Rejection:** The worry that being too ambitious or too vocal will lead to rejection causes you to second-guess yourself, avoiding risks or actions that could propel you forward.
- **Missed Opportunities for Leadership:** When you hide your brilliance to avoid being "too much," you miss opportunities to lead and influence others. You may shy away from roles, projects, or initiatives where your input could make a huge difference.
- **Perpetuating Societal Norms:** The fear of being "too much" is rooted in societal conditioning that limits women's freedom to be fully themselves. This continues the cycle of women being told to shrink, which limits progress in gender equality and individual empowerment.

How to Identify It:

- **Hesitation to Share Your Ideas:** You hesitate to bring forward your boldest ideas or voice your opinion in meetings, afraid of being too pushy or stepping on others' toes.
- **Downplaying Achievements:** You minimize or downplay your successes in conversations to make others feel comfortable or avoid appearing arrogant.

- **Second-Guessing Your Presence:** You worry about how others perceive you, constantly overthinking how you come across in professional or social situations.
- **Fear of Labels:** You worry about being labeled as "too aggressive," "too ambitious," or "too much" in a way that might negatively affect your reputation or relationships.
- **Suppressing Your Confidence:** You find yourself apologizing for being confident or assertive, often shrinking in situations where you should confidently claim your space.

Ways to Overcome It:

1. **Own Your Power:** Embrace the full extent of your brilliance and power. The world needs more women who own their greatness, who step into leadership roles and challenge the status quo. Stop apologizing for being ambitious, confident, or driven. You have every right to take up space and share your ideas with the world.
2. **Stop Filtering Yourself:** Give yourself permission to speak up and share your thoughts, even if they are bold or unconventional. Whether it's in a meeting, a social setting, or your personal life, stop second-guessing your words. If you have a strong opinion or a great idea, let it be heard. Your voice matters.
3. **Ask Yourself: "Would a Man Worry About This?"** This is a powerful tool for checking your fears. Would a man hesitate to speak up in a meeting or take credit for a great idea? The answer is often no. I practice this one with my husband often. When I'm running into any confidence issue, I ask my husband what he thinks about it, and he almost always tells me it's not a big deal and that men never think like this. If the fear of being "too much" is holding you back, ask yourself if the situation would be different if you were a man. This can

help you realize that your concerns are often rooted in societal conditioning rather than reality.
4. **Celebrate Your Boldness:** Recognize that being bold is not a flaw but a strength. Celebrate the moments when you stand up for yourself or take charge of a situation. Acknowledge that these actions bring value to your life and the lives of others around you.
5. **Challenge Societal Norms:** Start questioning the societal norms that make you feel like you have to shrink. The next time you find yourself holding back, remind yourself that the world needs your voice, ideas, and leadership. You are breaking barriers and paving the way for future generations of women to step into their full power.
6. **Seek Support from Like-Minded Women:** Surround yourself with women who encourage you to show up as your true self. Find a community that celebrates your ambition and confidence rather than making you feel like you need to apologize for it. When you have the support of others who understand your journey, it becomes easier to stand tall in your own power.
7. **Embrace Your Unique Strengths:** Recognize that your drive, ambition, and brilliance are qualities that set you apart and make you unique. Stop comparing yourself to others and celebrate what makes you different. Your presence is needed, and your energy is a gift.

The fear of being "too much" is a powerful roadblock that keeps so many women from fully stepping into their potential. It causes us to shrink, second-guess ourselves, and suppress our brilliance. But when we stop apologizing for who we are and start owning our power, we unlock our true potential. We create space for ourselves to lead, to share our ideas, and to make an impact. By overcoming this fear, we not only step into our greatness but also pave the way for other women to do the same. You are not too much—you're exactly what the world needs.

Roadblock #4: The Superwoman Complex

Let's talk about **overfunctioning**—aka, the belief that **you have to do everything, for everyone, all the time.**

We are so used to being the ones who hold it all together—the careers, the families, the relationships, the social calendars. And somewhere along the way, we internalized the idea that if we don't do it, no one else will. The Superwoman Complex is the belief that you have to be everything to everyone all the time—at work, at home, in your relationships, and in your personal life. It's the idea that if something needs to be done, you're the one who must do it, and if you don't, it won't get done at all, or it won't get done "right." This belief stems from a deep sense of responsibility and a fear that if you don't carry the weight, everything will fall apart. Over time, this mentality becomes ingrained, and you begin to operate from a place of constant doing, neglecting your needs and becoming overwhelmed by the never-ending demands on your time and energy.

How This Gets in the Way:

The Superwoman Complex can limit your growth and well-being in many ways:

- **Chronic Overwork:** Taking on everything yourself leads to exhaustion, burnout, and an inability to focus on what truly matters. You're spreading yourself too thin, and your productivity, quality of work, and personal fulfillment suffer in the process.
- **Difficulty Delegating:** The belief that you must do it all means you rarely ask for help or delegate tasks, which

causes unnecessary stress and prevents others from stepping up.
- **Resentment and Burnout:** Constantly meeting the needs of others while neglecting your own can lead to resentment. You might find yourself emotionally drained, frustrated, or even bitter because you're carrying so much, and no one seems to notice or appreciate it.
- **Lack of Boundaries:** The Superwoman Complex makes it difficult to say "no" or set clear boundaries because you feel like letting others down will somehow reflect poorly on you. As a result, you may become overcommitted and overwhelmed.
- **Inability to Enjoy Rest:** You may feel guilty or anxious when you're not being productive, unable to truly relax because you think you should always be doing something. This can erode your mental and physical well-being.

How to Identify It:

- **Reluctance to Ask for Help:** You rarely ask for assistance or even acknowledge when you need it because you believe it's your responsibility to take on everything.
- **Taking on More Than You Can Handle:** You constantly accept more tasks at work or at home, even if they stretch you too thin because you believe that if you don't do them, no one else will.
- **Guilt Around Rest:** You feel guilty when you're resting, taking a break, or not actively working toward a goal. You think that if you're not constantly busy, you're not being productive or valuable.
- **Difficulty Setting Boundaries:** You struggle to say "no" to requests, whether it's from colleagues, family, or friends. You don't want to disappoint others, so you end up saying

"yes" to too many things, even at the expense of your own well-being.
- **Feeling Overwhelmed or Burned Out:** You feel constantly overwhelmed by the demands placed on you, and when you try to relax, your mind is still racing with tasks you think you need to do.

Ways to Overcome It:
1. **Delegate Relentlessly:** Just because you're capable of doing everything doesn't mean you should. Delegate tasks at work and at home to free up space for the things that only you can do. Trust that others are more than capable of stepping up, and that doing so not only relieves your burden but empowers them to contribute as well. Sure, it may not be to the caliber that you would do it at first, but over time, you give them the opportunity to grow and improve, and you have one less thing to worry about!
2. **Let Go of Guilt:** Rest is essential for long-term success, not a sign of weakness. Saying no to requests or cutting back on obligations is not selfish—it's self-care. Let go of the guilt around taking time for yourself and recognize that you're helping yourself and improving your ability to serve others when you're well-rested and rejuvenated.
3. **Remember, You Are Not a Machine:** Burnout is not a badge of honor. It's a warning sign that you're pushing yourself too far. Listen to your body and mind when they signal that you need a break. Taking care of yourself allows you to perform better, think clearer, and maintain the energy needed to meet your responsibilities.
4. **Set Clear Boundaries:** Establish boundaries that support you. Say no when necessary, and be clear about your limits with others. Setting boundaries is not about rejecting

others, but about protecting your time and energy so you can show up as your best self.
5. **Reframe Your Identity:** Your worth is not determined by how much you do or give. Start to recognize that you are valuable simply because you are you, not because you are constantly busy or doing for others. Embrace the idea that it's OK to rest, ask for help, and take care of yourself without feeling guilty.
6. **Prioritize Your Well-Being:** Make self-care a priority, not an afterthought. Whether it's through exercise, mindfulness, or hobbies, ensure that you're taking time each day to nurture yourself. When you take care of yourself, you're better equipped to handle the demands of your work and personal life.
7. **Celebrate Your Contributions without Overworking:** Acknowledge your accomplishments and contributions, but recognize that you don't need to overfunction to feel proud of what you've done. You are enough just as you are, and your value isn't dependent on doing everything.

The Superwoman Complex is a common roadblock for women who have internalized the idea that they must do everything, all the time, for everyone. While it may seem like the path to success, it often leads to exhaustion, resentment, and burnout. By learning to delegate, let go of guilt, and set boundaries, you can break free from the cycle of overfunctioning. Remember that your worth is not tied to how much you do, but to who you are. By caring for yourself and acknowledging your need for rest and help, you'll be able to show up more effectively and authentically in every aspect of your life.

Roadblock #5: Fear of Failure (Or Success)

We don't just fear failure. We fear **what happens if we actually succeed.**

Success means change. It means stepping into a new version of yourself. It means people having **opinions** about you.

And sometimes, staying where you are—even if it's unfulfilling—feels safer than stepping into the unknown. We often think of fear as something that only holds us back from failure, but what if I told you that fear can also stem from the very idea of succeeding? Success brings with it a whole new set of challenges—new responsibilities, new expectations, and often, new opinions from others. Stepping into success can mean stepping into the unknown, which can feel overwhelming. Success means growth, and growth means change. Sometimes, the comfort of staying where you are feels safer than the uncertainty of what success might bring, even if it's unfulfilling. This fear—of failing or succeeding—can keep us stuck in situations that no longer serve us, holding us back from stepping into our true potential.

How This Gets in the Way:

The fear of both failure and success can create a cycle that keeps you from progressing:

- **Self-Sabotage:** The fear of success can cause you to delay or actively sabotage opportunities that would push you forward. You may find yourself procrastinating, overthinking, or talking yourself out of opportunities that could help you grow.
- **Fear of Outgrowing Relationships:** Success may bring changes that cause you to outgrow certain relationships, whether they're friendships, family dynamics, or professional connections. This fear of change can hold you back from pursuing success or lead you to stay in stagnant situations.
- **Staying Stuck:** The comfort of the familiar can be incredibly enticing, even if it's no longer serving you. The fear of the

unknown that comes with success can make you cling to situations, relationships, or jobs that no longer align with your goals or values simply because they feel safe.
- **Resistance to Change:** You may resist change because you fear what others will think or how your new success will impact your life. This fear can make you stay in a cycle of comfort rather than pushing yourself to evolve and grow.

How to Identify It:

- **Avoiding New Opportunities:** You hesitate to take on new opportunities or challenges, even when you know they could help you grow or move forward. You find yourself procrastinating or making excuses to avoid change.
- **Overthinking Potential Success:** You worry more about the consequences of success—such as how it will affect your relationships or your lifestyle—than about taking action toward achieving your goals.
- **Staying in Unfulfilling Situations:** You remain stuck in situations, careers, or relationships that no longer serve you because the fear of change feels too overwhelming, even though staying where you are feels unfulfilling.
- **Perfectionism:** You struggle with perfectionism because you're afraid of taking the wrong step or making a mistake that could derail your success, so you avoid moving forward altogether.
- **Discomfort with Growth:** You notice discomfort or resistance when thinking about what success might bring, including the expectations or changes that will come with it.

Ways to Overcome It:

1. **Reframe Fear As Excitement:** Fear and excitement are processed the same way in the brain, so instead of saying, "I'm scared," try telling yourself, "I'm excited." This simple

shift can help you view the fear surrounding success as a positive indicator that you're moving toward growth and new opportunities.

2. **Normalize Growth:** Understand that you are meant to evolve and grow. Success will require you to adapt, and not everyone will be able to come along with you on your journey. That's OK. Recognize that growth involves letting go of old identities, relationships, and situations that no longer align with who you are becoming.

3. **Take the First Step:** Rather than waiting for the "perfect" moment or for everything to fall into place, take one small step toward your goals. Once you start moving, momentum will carry you forward.

4. **Use Fear As a Guide:** If something scares you, it's often a sign that you're stepping into new territory, which is a necessary part of growth. Rather than running from fear, move toward it. Lean into the discomfort, and trust that it is signaling that you're pushing boundaries and expanding your potential.

5. **Trust Yourself:** Remind yourself of your successes and the challenges you've already overcome. You've faced uncertainty before and emerged stronger. Trust that you can handle whatever comes your way and that you will adapt and grow through any challenges.

6. **Visualize the Positive Aspects of Success:** Instead of focusing on the potential challenges or discomforts that success may bring, focus on the benefits—the freedom, fulfillment, and impact you can create by stepping into your full potential. By visualizing the positive side of success, you can ease some of the fear and embrace the change it brings.

7. **Create a Supportive Environment:** Surround yourself with people who support your growth and encourage your

success. When you have a strong support network, it becomes easier to navigate the fear of success and the changes it brings. They can help you stay grounded and remind you that you are capable of handling the next steps.

The fear of both failure and success is a powerful roadblock that can keep you from achieving your full potential. While failure can feel like a threat, success can bring challenges, such as change and the unknown. However, it's important to recognize that fear is not an enemy but a guide to growth. When you move toward fear, you move toward your potential. By reframing your fear, taking action, and trusting yourself, you can overcome this roadblock and step into the success that is waiting for you. Fear doesn't have to stop you; it can be a sign that you're on the path to something greater.

Fear is inevitable. But fear does not have to be the enemy. Fear signals growth. If you're afraid, it means you're pushing boundaries. The key is to act despite the fear.

Roadblock #6: Not Getting the Support You Need

You cannot do this alone. Period.

One of the most overlooked roadblocks for high-achieving women is the lack of support. Women need a partner who helps drive their success, not one who simply tolerates it. If you don't have the support you need—from a spouse, partner, family, or colleagues—it can feel like you're carrying the weight of the world alone.

Success is not a solo journey. As high-achieving women, we often feel the pressure to do it all on our own—managing our careers, families, relationships, and personal goals. However, this mindset can be a major roadblock, especially when we lack the support system. Whether it's from a partner, family, friends, or colleagues, support is essential for growth and success. You need people who not only tolerate your ambitions but actively help drive them. Without the right support, you can quickly feel overwhelmed, isolated, and burdened by the weight of carrying everything alone. Success is much more sustainable when it's shared and supported by those around you.

How This Gets in the Way:

Lack of support can affect every area of your life, causing unnecessary stress and preventing you from reaching your full potential:

- **Emotional Exhaustion:** When you don't have support, you're left to manage everything yourself. This constant mental and emotional load can quickly lead to burnout, as you're trying to juggle multiple responsibilities without help or understanding.
- **Guilt and Justification:** If you always feel the need to justify your career ambitions to your partner, family, or friends, it's a sign that you lack the emotional backing you need to move forward confidently. This guilt can hold you back from fully embracing your potential or pursuing opportunities.
- **Taking on More Responsibility:** Without proper support, you may take on more than your fair share at work or home, which only amplifies feelings of overwhelm and resentment. This can prevent you from focusing on the things that matter most or advancing in your career.
- **Lack of Confidence in Major Decisions:** When you're not supported in the big decisions or changes you want to make, it can lead to self-doubt or hesitation. You may second-guess your choices or feel unsure of whether you should proceed without the backing of those around you.

How to Identify It:

- **Justifying Your Ambitions:** You feel like you're constantly having to explain why your career goals, ambitions, or time commitments matter to others, particularly your partner or family.
- **Carrying the Weight Alone:** You take on more than your share of household or work responsibilities because you don't have the help or support you need from others.
- **Lack of Trust in Key Decisions:** You feel unsupported when making significant decisions or changes in your career or personal life, leading to indecision or hesitation.
- **Feeling Overwhelmed by the Demands of Others:** You feel constantly drained by the demands of others and struggle to find the time or energy to pursue your own goals.
- **Resentment toward Unsupportive People:** You notice frustration or resentment toward those who don't understand or support your ambitions, which may affect your relationships or sense of self-worth.

Ways to Overcome It:

1. **Have the Hard Conversations:** Clear communication is key. Take the time to sit down with your partner, family, or colleagues, and share exactly what you need. Be honest about the support you're seeking—whether it's emotional, practical, or strategic—and explain how their support will help you achieve your goals. Having an open and honest conversation is often the first step toward gaining the support you need.
2. **Surround Yourself with the Right People:** Seek mentors, coaches, and a network of women who understand your journey and are ready to lift you up. The right people can provide guidance, accountability, and encouragement,

helping you feel more supported in your ambitions. Find those who believe in your potential and can help you navigate challenges with confidence.

3. **Let Go of Those Who Drain You:** Not everyone around you will be a supportive presence, and that's all right. Suppose someone is consistently undermining your ambitions, making you feel guilty, or draining your energy. In that case, it may be time to reevaluate their role in your life. Set boundaries with individuals who don't support your growth, and prioritize relationships that nurture your success.

4. **Build a Supportive Home Environment:** If you feel unsupported by your partner or family, work together to create a more supportive environment. This may involve redistributing household responsibilities, clarifying expectations, or setting aside time to discuss your goals and needs. A healthy, supportive partnership is essential for personal and professional success.

5. **Delegate at Work and Home:** Don't hesitate to delegate tasks. This frees up your time and energy to focus on the big picture—your goals and ambitions. By delegating, you show others that it's all right to ask for help, and you don't have to do it all on your own.

6. **Invest in Your Growth:** Surround yourself with a team of people who will push you forward. Whether hiring a coach, joining a mastermind group, or seeking networking opportunities, investing in your growth can provide the tools, resources, and support you need to succeed.

7. **Seek Emotional and Practical Balance:** Ensure you're getting the emotional support you need while creating practical structures to help you manage your responsibilities. It's about finding a rhythm that allows you

to thrive in every area of your life with the backing of those around you.

Not getting the support you need is a roadblock that can prevent you from reaching your full potential and leave you feeling overwhelmed, isolated, and stuck. You cannot do it all alone—success requires collaboration and the right people who understand and support your ambitions. By having the hard conversations, surrounding yourself with empowering individuals, and letting go of those who drain your energy, you can create the support system necessary for your growth and success. When you have the right support, you'll not only feel more confident in your decisions but also experience the freedom to pursue your dreams and achieve your fullest potential.

Roadblock #7: Limiting Beliefs

Your mind is either your greatest asset or your biggest limitation. The stories you tell yourself determine what's possible. Limiting beliefs are the negative, often unconscious stories you tell yourself about your abilities, worth, or potential. These beliefs are often formed from past experiences, societal expectations, or fear of failure. When you believe that you are incapable, unworthy, or undeserving of success, you unconsciously limit your growth and hold yourself back from pursuing bigger goals. These beliefs can be so ingrained that you don't even realize they're influencing your decisions, actions, or the way you see yourself.

How This Gets in the Way:

Limiting beliefs can have a profound impact on your success and overall well-being:

- **Self-Doubt:** You may doubt your own capabilities, even when you have proof of your success. This can lead to

hesitation, indecision, and a lack of confidence in your abilities.
- **Fear of Making Mistakes:** Limiting beliefs often lead to perfectionism and an intense fear of making the wrong choice. This causes you to second-guess major decisions and miss opportunities out of fear of failure.
- **Setting Smaller Goals:** Deep down, you may not believe you can achieve more, so you set smaller or more "realistic" goals to avoid disappointment. This keeps you stuck in your comfort zone and prevents you from reaching your full potential.
- **Avoiding Challenges:** The fear that you're not good enough or capable enough can prevent you from taking on challenges, making it harder to grow in your career or personal life. You may avoid stepping out of your comfort zone, which is necessary for growth.
- **Imposter Syndrome:** Limiting beliefs can lead to imposter syndrome, where you feel like a fraud or that you don't truly deserve your success, even when you've earned it. This internal conflict can create stress, insecurity, and a lack of fulfillment.

How to Identify It:

- **Self-Doubt:** You frequently question your abilities or downplay your achievements, even when others recognize your success.
- **Second-Guessing Decisions:** You hesitate to make big decisions, fearing you might make the wrong choice or regret your actions later.
- **Small Goals:** You set goals that feel safe and achievable, avoiding any big dreams or aspirations because you don't believe you can achieve them.

- **Negative Self-Talk:** You tell yourself things like, "I'm not good enough," "I can't do this," or "I'll never be able to handle this," even when there's evidence to the contrary.
- **Comparing Yourself to Others:** You compare your progress to others, feeling inadequate or like you're falling behind despite your successes.

Ways to Overcome It:

1. **Rewrite the Narrative:** Identify the limiting beliefs that are holding you back and consciously replace them with empowering ones. For example, if you believe you're not capable of success, replace that with the belief, "I am fully capable of achieving my goals." Challenge these negative beliefs by recognizing them for what they are—old stories that no longer serve you—and consciously rewrite them with a positive, growth-oriented narrative.
2. **Act "As If":** Show up today as the woman who already has what you want. If you believe you're incapable of leading a team or handling a new responsibility, start acting as if you already are in that position. Take bold steps, speak with confidence, and make decisions with the belief that you're fully capable. This shift in mindset will help you break free from your limiting beliefs and align your actions with your true potential.
3. **Surround Yourself with Possibility:** Start consuming content that challenges your thinking and exposes you to new possibilities. Listen to podcasts, read books, and follow women who inspire you and challenge your current mindset. Surrounding yourself with stories of others who have broken through their limiting beliefs will reinforce the idea that you can do the same. Make sure to seek out people who lift you up and expand your vision of what's possible.

4. **Practice Affirmations:** Use daily affirmations to reinforce your new, empowering beliefs. Write down and repeat statements such as, "I am worthy of success," "I am capable of achieving my dreams," and "I trust myself to make the right decisions." These affirmations help shift your mindset over time and reprogram your subconscious to believe in your potential.
5. **Take Action Despite Fear:** The best way to overcome limiting beliefs is through action. Even if you feel scared or unsure, take steps toward your goals. Small actions lead to bigger results, and the more you push past your fears, the more your confidence will grow. Each step will prove that you are capable of much more than your limiting beliefs would have you think.
6. **Challenge Your Comfort Zone:** Whenever you catch yourself playing small or limiting your goals, challenge yourself to step outside your comfort zone. Start by taking on something that scares you, even if it's just a small step. The more you step into the unknown, the more you'll realize your strength and capability.

Limiting beliefs are powerful roadblocks that can keep you stuck in patterns of self-doubt and fear. However, these beliefs are not truths—they are just stories you've told yourself based on past experiences or societal conditioning. You can break free from these limitations by rewriting the narrative, acting as if you already have what you want, and surrounding yourself with people and content that expand your thinking. Your mind is your greatest asset; with the right mindset, you can achieve far more than you ever thought possible. Shift your beliefs, take bold action, and watch as your potential unfolds before you.

Roadblock #8: Shame and Guilt

Shame and guilt are powerful emotions that can hold you back from moving forward in life. While guilt focuses on feeling bad about actions or choices you've made, shame convinces you that you are inherently flawed or unworthy of success and happiness. Guilt keeps you trapped in the past, while shame keeps you from even trying to move forward because you feel like you don't deserve better. These emotions can cause you to second-guess yourself, sabotage your progress, and prevent you from fully embracing your potential. Letting go of these feelings is essential for reclaiming your power and moving toward the life you deserve.

How This Gets in the Way:

Shame and guilt can keep you trapped in negative thought patterns, making it difficult to take the necessary steps to achieve your goals:

- **Self-Sabotage:** Guilt can lead you to feel undeserving of success, causing you to sabotage your own progress. You might downplay your accomplishments, hesitate to take bold steps, or avoid opportunities because you feel unworthy.
- **Living in the Past:** When you replay past mistakes over and over, you keep yourself stuck in a cycle of regret and self-blame. This prevents you from learning from the experience and moving forward with new insights.
- **Perfectionism:** Shame often leads to perfectionism. You hold yourself to impossibly high standards, believing that anything less than perfect is a failure. When you fall short, you beat yourself up, deepening your feelings of inadequacy and keeping you from progressing.
- **Fear of Success:** Shame can also create a fear of success because you may feel unworthy of achieving your dreams

or fear that others will judge you. This can hold you back from stepping into your full potential, as you unconsciously believe you don't deserve it.

How to Identify It:

- **Guilt About Prioritizing Yourself:** You feel guilty when you focus on your career, personal growth, or self-care as if taking time for yourself is selfish or wrong.
- **Replaying Past Mistakes:** You constantly replay mistakes or missed opportunities in your mind, ruminating over what went wrong instead of using those moments as learning experiences.
- **Self-Criticism:** You set unrealistically high standards for yourself and feel like a failure when you don't meet them. You beat yourself up for every small mistake or perceived flaw.
- **Feeling Unworthy of Success:** You feel like you don't deserve success, happiness, or fulfillment, and this belief prevents you from fully embracing the opportunities that come your way.
- **Fear of Being Judged:** You avoid putting yourself out there because you're worried about how others will perceive you, or you feel like your success will make others uncomfortable or envious.

Ways to Overcome It:

1. **Release the Guilt:** Understand that your success does not take away from anyone else. You have every right to prioritize your goals and ambitions. By achieving success, you are not diminishing others; you're inspiring them. Let go of the guilt that keeps you from stepping into your power and pursuing your dreams.

2. **Forgive Yourself:** Mistakes are not life sentences; they are lessons. Everyone makes mistakes, and they are essential for growth. Instead of holding onto guilt and shame about your past, forgive yourself. Use your mistakes as learning tools to help you grow and improve rather than allowing them to define you or your future.
3. **Remember, You Deserve Success:** You are worthy of achieving your goals and living the life you desire. Your success is not contingent on making others comfortable or meeting their expectations. You do not have to shrink yourself to make others feel good about themselves. You are not responsible for the comfort of others at the expense of your own dreams.
4. **Practice Self-Compassion:** Be kind to yourself when you make mistakes or fall short of your goals. Treat yourself with the same compassion and understanding you would offer a close friend.
5. **Shift Your Perspective on Success:** Reframe success as an opportunity to grow, learn, and contribute to the world. When you feel shame or guilt about pursuing your dreams, remind yourself that your success can positively impact others. You have the power to use your achievements to inspire, support, and uplift others.
6. **Surround Yourself with Supportive People:** Surround yourself with people who believe in your potential and encourage you to pursue your dreams. Positive relationships are essential for building self-worth and overcoming guilt and shame.
7. **Celebrate Your Wins:** Take time to acknowledge and celebrate your accomplishments, no matter how small. This reinforces the idea that you are worthy of success and helps you build confidence in your ability to achieve more.

8. **Reframe Your Inner Dialogue:** Pay attention to the way you speak to yourself. Replace self-critical thoughts with affirmations that affirm your worth and potential. Practice saying, "I am worthy of success," "I forgive myself for past mistakes," and "I deserve to live a fulfilling life."

Shame and guilt can be debilitating roadblocks that hold you back from reaching your full potential. These emotions keep you stuck in the past, unable to move forward and fully embrace the life you deserve. By releasing guilt, forgiving yourself for past mistakes, and remembering that you are worthy of success, you can begin to heal and step into your power. Success is not something to be ashamed of—it's something you deserve. Let go of the limiting beliefs that hold you back, and allow yourself to fully embrace the endless possibilities that lie ahead. You are enough, and you are worthy of every success that comes your way.

Roadblock #9: Unreasonable Expectations

Everything will take longer than you think it should. Expect it.

As high-achieving women, it's easy to set unrealistic expectations for ourselves. We often expect things to happen faster than they realistically can, pushing ourselves to achieve more in less time. Whether it's building a business, advancing in your career, or personal growth, the road to success is rarely a straight line or quick process. Expecting instant results or perfection can lead to frustration, disappointment, and burnout. Understanding that progress takes time and that setbacks are a natural part of the journey is crucial for sustaining long-term success and maintaining mental and emotional well-being.

How This Gets in the Way:

Unreasonable expectations can cause you to undermine your progress in several ways:

- **Frustration and Disappointment:** When things take longer than expected, it can lead to feelings of frustration or disappointment. If you're not meeting self-imposed deadlines, you may feel like you're failing, even if you're making significant progress.
- **Burnout:** Pushing yourself to meet unrealistic timelines can cause stress and exhaustion. You may sacrifice self-care, family time, or mental health in an attempt to meet goals that are simply too ambitious for the timeframe you've set.
- **Perfectionism:** Unreasonable expectations often tie into perfectionism, as we set high standards that are impossible to meet. When we don't meet those standards, we feel like we haven't achieved enough, hindering our sense of accomplishment and preventing us from moving forward.
- **Avoidance of Challenges:** The fear of not meeting unrealistic timelines can cause you to avoid difficult but necessary tasks, creating unnecessary delays and preventing you from learning or growing through challenges.

How to Identify It:

- **Frustration with Progress:** You frequently feel frustrated or disappointed when things don't go as planned or take longer than expected.
- **Setting Unrealistic Deadlines:** You tend to set too aggressive deadlines and don't allow room for the natural ebb and flow of life, leading to constant pressure.
- **Procrastination or Avoidance:** You delay taking action because you fear not being able to meet the expectations

you've set for yourself, which causes you to avoid moving forward.
- **Feeling Stuck:** You feel paralyzed when things take longer than you expect, thinking that you're behind or not accomplishing enough.

Ways to Overcome It:

1. **Adjust Your Timelines:** Understand that success is a long game. Things will inevitably take longer than you anticipate, and that's fine. Adjust your expectations to reflect reality, and build in buffer time for setbacks or unexpected challenges. This reduces pressure and allows you to stay focused on the big picture rather than getting discouraged by short-term delays.
2. **Measure Progress:** Celebrate every step forward, no matter how small. Every action you take, no matter how incremental, is a step toward your goal. Acknowledge your accomplishments and milestones, even if they don't match the initial timeline you set.
3. **Create Realistic Milestones:** Break down your larger goals into smaller, more achievable milestones. This allows you to track progress more easily and gives you a sense of accomplishment along the way. Setting more manageable goals reduces the likelihood of feeling overwhelmed or disappointed by your progress.
4. **Embrace the Learning Process:** Understand that growth and success come with challenges. When things take longer than expected, see it as an opportunity for learning rather than a setback. Embrace the lessons that come with delays or obstacles, as they will contribute to your long-term growth and success.
5. **Build in Flexibility:** Leave room for flexibility in your plans. Life can be unpredictable, and success is rarely a straight

path. Allow space for adjustments in your timeline when things don't go as planned. Flexibility helps you stay resilient and adaptable, making it easier to bounce back when things take longer than expected.
6. **Practice Patience:** Cultivate patience with yourself and the process. Success takes time, and every step forward, no matter how slow, is progress. Trust that consistency and persistence will pay off over time, even if it doesn't happen as quickly as you'd like.
7. **Focus on Long-Term Vision:** Keep your eyes on the bigger picture. Remind yourself why you're doing what you're doing, and focus on the long-term rewards rather than short-term delays. This helps you stay motivated and grounded, even when things take longer than anticipated.
8. **Seek Accountability and Support:** Share your goals and progress with a mentor, coach, or trusted friend who can help you stay grounded in realistic expectations. Sometimes, external perspectives can help you recognize when you're setting yourself up for unnecessary stress.

Unreasonable expectations can be a significant roadblock to success, causing frustration, burnout, and a lack of progress. By adjusting your timelines, and building flexibility into your plans, you can overcome this roadblock and stay on track for long-term success. Remember that growth and success are a journey, not a race, and every step you take is valuable. Be patient with yourself, celebrate your progress, and trust that consistency will lead to the success you desire.

Roadblock #10: Energy-Sucking People & Haters

Some people want to see you win. Others want to see you struggle. Energy-draining individuals thrive on negativity and will do everything they can to slow you down, whether consciously or subconsciously. These people can show up as friends, family, or even colleagues.

There are people who will lift you up and cheer you on, but unfortunately, there are also those who thrive on negativity and will do everything they can—consciously or subconsciously—to drain your energy and slow you down. These individuals may appear in various forms, such as friends, family members, colleagues, or acquaintances. Whether they criticize your goals, undermine your progress, or simply bring negativity into your life, their influence can significantly hinder your ability to achieve your dreams. The challenge is recognizing these energy-draining people and protecting yourself from their impact so that you can focus on your own success and well-being.

How This Gets in the Way:

Energy-sucking people can have a profound impact on your ability to move forward:

- **Self-Doubt and Negative Thinking:** When you interact with people who bring negativity into your life, it can lead to self-doubt or cause you to question your decisions. This can undermine your confidence and make you second-guess your abilities and potential.
- **Emotional Drain:** Negative people often leave you feeling drained, exhausted, and emotionally spent after spending time with them. This can affect your mental and emotional health, leaving you with less energy to focus on your goals or pursue your passions.
- **Distraction from Your Goals:** When you're surrounded by unsupportive individuals who actively try to bring you down, it can divert your attention away from your ambitions. Their negativity becomes a distraction that keeps you from staying focused and moving forward.

- **Stagnation or Regression:** The constant negativity can create an environment where you feel stuck or, even worse, as though you are regressing. Energy-sucking individuals can make you feel like your goals are unrealistic or unworthy, preventing you from progressing and reaching your full potential.

How to Identify It:

- **Post-Interaction Exhaustion:** After spending time with certain people, you feel mentally and emotionally drained. These interactions leave you feeling depleted and questioning your self-worth or decisions.
- **Negative or Critical Conversations:** The people around you frequently criticize your goals, aspirations, or ideas. They may belittle your achievements or focus on what could go wrong rather than offering constructive feedback.
- **Lack of Support:** Instead of offering encouragement, energy-draining people may act indifferent or even hostile toward your success. They may express doubt about your abilities or minimize your accomplishments.
- **Constant Drama or Conflict:** These individuals often bring drama or unnecessary conflict into your life, creating chaos and pulling you away from your focus on your goals and well-being.
- **Feeling Like You're "Not Enough":** After interacting with them, you start to feel like you're not doing enough, not capable enough, or that your dreams are unrealistic, even if those thoughts didn't exist before.

Ways to Overcome It:

1. **Identify the Drainers:** Pay attention to how you feel after interacting with certain people. Do you leave conversations feeling energized and motivated, or do you feel drained and

doubtful? If certain people consistently make you feel worse about yourself or your goals, it's a sign they may be energy-drainers. Recognize these patterns, and take note of whom you need to limit your exposure to.

2. **Set Clear Boundaries:** You are not obligated to entertain negativity or engage with people who undermine your success. Set boundaries by limiting your interactions with energy-draining individuals. Politely but firmly enforce those boundaries by making it clear when you're unavailable for negativity or criticism. This might mean declining invitations, changing the subject during conversations, or simply distancing yourself from certain relationships.

3. **Protect Your Time and Energy:** Be mindful of where you invest your time and energy. Every minute spent with negative, unsupportive people is a minute you're not investing in your growth and success. Prioritize your mental and emotional well-being by creating space for activities and relationships that lift you up rather than drain you.

4. **Find Your Supporters:** Surround yourself with people who genuinely want to see you succeed. Seek friends, family, colleagues, mentors, or a community that uplifts you, encourages, and supports your goals. These people will not only provide positivity and motivation but will also hold you accountable and help you navigate challenges with a constructive mindset.

5. **Minimize Contact with Haters:** While it's not always possible to eliminate every energy-draining person from your life, you can minimize your contact with them. Limit interactions to what is absolutely necessary, and always protect your emotional space. If you must interact, keep

conversations focused on neutral topics to avoid emotional draining.
6. **Develop Emotional Resilience:** Strengthen your emotional resilience so that you're less affected by negativity. Practice mindfulness, self-compassion, and positive self-talk to help you stay grounded in your worth and goals, regardless of what others say or think. When you learn to protect your emotional well-being, external negativity has less power over you.
7. **Practice Gratitude and Positivity:** Focus on the positive aspects of your life and the people who support you. Regularly practice gratitude for your supportive relationships and the progress you're making toward your goals. This helps shift your mindset and reinforces your positive environment.
8. **Limit Social Media Exposure:** In addition to physical interactions, energy-draining people can also show up on social media. If there are individuals or accounts that constantly drain your energy or feed into negativity, unfollow, mute, or block them. Curate your online environment to be one that supports your personal and professional growth.

Energy-sucking people and haters can significantly impact your ability to stay focused, confident, and motivated as you work toward your goals. By identifying these individuals, setting clear boundaries, and surrounding yourself with supportive, uplifting people, you can protect your time, energy, and mental health. You deserve to be surrounded by individuals who empower you to succeed, not drag you down. Prioritize relationships that nurture your growth and success, and let go of those that hinder your progress. When you cultivate a supportive environment, you'll find it easier to stay focused, driven, and inspired to reach your full potential.

Roadblock #11: Victim Mindset

No one is coming to save you. You are responsible for your own success. Playing the victim means giving away your power and waiting for someone else to fix your problems.

A victim mindset is one where you feel powerless, believing that external circumstances, other people, or the world at large are responsible for your struggles or lack of success. This mindset keeps you stuck in a cycle of blame, where you wait for someone else to come along and fix things for you. However, the truth is that no one is coming to save you, and you are the one who holds the key to your success. Embracing personal responsibility is empowering and allows you to take control of your life and make the necessary changes to move forward. A victim mindset drains your energy and limits your potential, keeping you from embracing your power and finding solutions to your problems.

How This Gets in the Way:

The victim mindset can prevent you from making progress in various ways:

- **Passivity and Inaction:** Believing that you are at the mercy of external factors or other people can make you passive and unwilling to take action. This inaction keeps you stuck and prevents you from moving forward toward your goals.
- **Blaming External Factors:** When you focus on blaming your circumstances, your boss, your family, or anything outside of yourself, you give away your power. This external focus distracts you from the actions you can take to change your situation.

- **Feelings of Helplessness:** The victim mindset creates feelings of helplessness and hopelessness. You may feel like success is out of your control, which leads to a lack of motivation or desire to take risks and make changes.
- **Stagnation:** By focusing on what's wrong, what's not working, or what others have done to prevent your success, you become stuck in a cycle of negativity that prevents you from moving forward.
- **Lack of Accountability:** A victim mindset often leads to avoiding personal responsibility. When things go wrong, the tendency is to blame others rather than reflect on what you can do differently or how you can change your approach.

How to Identify It:

- **Blaming Others or External Circumstances:** You frequently blame others, the economy, or your past for where you are today instead of acknowledging your role in your current situation.
- **Feeling Powerless or Helpless:** You often feel like your success is dependent on factors outside of your control, leading to feelings of helplessness or frustration.
- **Resisting Change or Growth:** You're hesitant to take responsibility for your situation and avoid making changes. Instead, you wait for someone or something to "fix" things for you.
- **Negative Self-Talk:** You may tell yourself things like, "Nothing ever works out for me," "I'll never be successful," or "Other people have it easier than I do," reinforcing the idea that you're a victim of your circumstances.
- **Fear of Failure:** The victim mindset can lead to a fear of failure because you believe that failure is proof that things

will never work out for you, rather than seeing it as part of the process of growth.

Ways to Overcome It:

1. **Take Full Ownership:** Shift your perspective from blaming external factors to taking responsibility for your situation. Instead of asking, "Why is this happening to me?" ask, "What can I do to change this situation?" Taking ownership of your circumstances allows you to reclaim your power and start taking actionable steps toward change.
2. **Reframe Challenges:** See setbacks and obstacles as opportunities for growth, not as proof that success is impossible for you. Reframing challenges helps you build resilience and learn from each experience, making you stronger and more capable of handling future difficulties. When something goes wrong, ask yourself, "What can I learn from this?" instead of "Why does this always happen to me?"
3. **Develop a Solution-Oriented Mindset:** Focus on finding ways forward rather than dwelling on what went wrong or what you can't control. Shift your thinking to identify solutions, resources, and steps you can take to make progress. Every problem has a solution—when you focus on solutions, you empower yourself to overcome obstacles and move toward your goals.
4. **Change Your Self-Talk:** Replace negative, victim-based self-talk with affirmations of empowerment and action. Instead of saying, "I can't do this," say, "I have the power to overcome this challenge." Positive self-talk reinforces a sense of control and self-efficacy, which motivates you to act and persist in the face of adversity.
5. **Cultivate Accountability:** Hold yourself accountable for your actions and outcomes. Take ownership of your choices

and recognize how they contribute to your progress or setbacks. When you take responsibility for your actions, you empower yourself to make necessary changes and take control of your future.

6. **Focus on What You Can Control:** While you can't control everything, you can control how you respond to challenges. Focus on the actions you can take, the changes you can make, and the decisions you can own. By focusing on what's within your control, you minimize the power external factors have over your success.
7. **Celebrate Small Wins:** Acknowledge your progress, even if it's small. Celebrating every step forward reinforces the belief that you are in control of your success and that your efforts are paying off. This builds confidence and momentum, helping you continue taking action.
8. **Surround Yourself with Empowering People:** Spend time with people who encourage you to take ownership of your life and support your efforts to grow. Avoid those who reinforce the victim mindset by focusing on problems instead of solutions.

The victim mindset is a powerful roadblock that can prevent you from moving forward and achieving your goals. It keeps you stuck in a cycle of blame, helplessness, and inaction. You can break free from this limiting belief by taking full ownership of your circumstances, reframing challenges as opportunities, and developing a solution-oriented mindset. Remember, you have the power to change your situation and create the success you desire. Focus on what you can control, take responsibility for your actions, and watch as you begin to take charge of your life and your future.

Roadblock #12: Comparison – The Thief of Joy

Comparison is a powerful roadblock that can derail your progress and steal your happiness. It's all too easy to look around at others and think they have it all together—whether it's their career, personal life, or accomplishments. But everyone has their unique journey, and comparing yours to someone else's is a surefire way to feel inadequate and disheartened. When you compare yourself to others, you lose sight of your strengths, progress, and individuality. Comparison breeds discontent and distracts you from focusing on your own path and celebrating your achievements.

In the age of social media, comparison is more prevalent than ever. We see the highlight reels of other people's lives and measure them against our behind-the-scenes struggles. But no one's journey is the same, and each person's timeline is different. The moment you stop comparing and start appreciating your growth, you'll find peace and fulfillment in your journey.

How This Gets in the Way:

Comparison can hinder your success and well-being in various ways:

- **Undermines Confidence:** When you constantly measure yourself against others, it's easy to feel like you're falling short. This erodes your self-confidence and makes you doubt your abilities, even if you've already made significant progress.
- **Distraction from Your Own Goals:** Comparing yourself to others shifts your focus from your aspirations to someone else's. This distraction keeps you from investing your energy into the things that truly matter to you.
- **Imposter Syndrome:** When you look at others and think they have it all figured out, you might feel like a fraud or that

you don't belong in your spaces. This feeling of inadequacy leads to imposter syndrome, where you doubt your worth despite your accomplishments.
- **Chronic Dissatisfaction:** Comparing yourself to others can lead to constant dissatisfaction. No matter how far you've come, someone else's success can make you feel like you're not doing enough or achieving at the same level.
- **Increased Anxiety:** The pressure to keep up with others can cause anxiety. The belief that you should be achieving the same things as someone else by a certain age or time can create unnecessary stress and pressure, making you feel like you're falling behind.

How to Identify It:

- **Frequent Negative Self-Talk:** You often find yourself thinking things like, "I'm not as successful as she is," or "I'll never be able to achieve what they have." This self-talk stems from comparing your life and progress to others.
- **Feeling Jealous or Envious:** When you see someone else succeeding, you feel envious or jealous instead of inspired. This is a clear sign that comparison is stealing your joy.
- **Focusing on Others' Successes:** You spend more time focusing on others' achievements and milestones than on your own. You might feel like you're always measuring your worth based on what others are doing.
- **Self-Doubt and Insecurity:** You often question your worth or abilities, wondering why you're not as accomplished or successful as those around you. You may also feel like you're not "good enough."
- **Avoiding Your Success:** You downplay or dismiss your achievements because you feel they don't measure up to the success of others.

Ways to Overcome It:

1. **Focus on Your Journey:** Remind yourself that your path is unique. No one else's timeline or journey will look like yours, and that's OK. Focus on where you are right now, and set goals that align with *your* vision and values, not someone else's.
2. **Celebrate Your Wins, Big and Small:** Take time to acknowledge and celebrate your successes, no matter how small they may seem. Every step forward is progress, and each achievement brings you closer to your goals. When you celebrate your wins, you reinforce the idea that your journey is valuable and worth celebrating.
3. **Limit Social Media Exposure:** Social media can be a major catalyst for comparison. Consider unfollowing or muting accounts that make you feel inadequate or trigger envy. Curate your feed to include people and content that inspire and uplift you rather than make you feel like you're falling behind.
4. **Practice Gratitude:** Take time daily to reflect on what you're grateful for. Focusing on what you already have—your talents, your progress, and the people who support you—helps shift your focus from what others are doing to what you're building for yourself.
5. **Reframe Your Thoughts:** When you catch yourself comparing, pause and reframe your thoughts. Instead of thinking, "I'm not as far along as she is," try thinking, "I'm proud of how far I've come, and I'm excited to keep growing." Reframing comparison into a positive affirmation helps you stay grounded in your own journey.
6. **Shift from Competition to Collaboration:** Instead of viewing others' success as a threat or something to envy, see it as inspiration. Embrace collaboration rather than

competition, and learn from others. You don't need to compete to succeed—there is enough success for everyone.

7. **Trust the Process:** Recognize that growth and success take time. Trust that the work you're putting in will pay off, even if it doesn't happen on the timeline you expect. Embrace the process rather than rushing toward the result. Every step you take is part of your unique story.
8. **Focus on Your Strengths:** Instead of comparing your weaknesses to others' strengths, focus on what you bring to the table. Recognize your special qualities, talents, and abilities that make you stand out in your own right. Celebrate what makes you different and how those differences can contribute to your success.

Comparison is the thief of joy, and it robs you of the ability to appreciate your growth and progress. It distracts you from your goals, breeds insecurity, and leads to chronic dissatisfaction. By focusing on your journey, celebrating your successes, and limiting exposure to negativity, you can break free from the trap of comparison. Remember, your path is distinctive, and there is room for your success alongside everyone else's. Stop measuring your worth against others, and start measuring it by your own standards and growth. The more you focus on your progress and embrace your individual journey, the more joyful and fulfilled you will become.

Taking Action: Identifying Your Roadblocks

Now that we've discussed some of the most common roadblocks, it's time to identify your personal obstacles so that you can begin to take action toward overcoming them. This section will help you reflect on your challenges, understand what's holding you back, and create a plan for moving forward with purpose and confidence.

Exercise 1: Where Are You Stuck?

Reflecting on where you feel stuck is the first step to uncovering which roadblocks are most relevant to your current journey. By acknowledging your struggles, you can make sense of them and find ways to move forward.

Questions to Reflect On:

1. **Which of these roadblocks resonates with you the most? Why?**
   Take a moment to think about the roadblocks discussed in the previous section. Which ones feel the most relevant to your current situation? Do you struggle with perfectionism, fear of failure, or setting unrealistic expectations for yourself? Write down which roadblock stood out to you, and explore why it resonates with you. Are there past experiences or current circumstances that make this roadblock feel especially challenging?

2. **Where in your life do you feel stuck or held back?**
   Identify the areas of your life where you're feeling stagnant. Is it in your career, personal relationships, health, or self-worth? Pinpoint where you feel limited and frustrated. Ask yourself: *What is the situation I'm avoiding or finding difficult to face? What has been stopping me from making the changes I desire?* Writing down these feelings can bring clarity about where you need to focus your energy.

3. **What stories are you telling yourself about why you can't move forward?**
   The stories we tell ourselves often hold the key to our limiting beliefs. Are you telling yourself that you're not ready, not worthy, or that others won't support you? These internal narratives can keep you stuck. Reflect on the

thoughts or self-talk that come up when you think about making progress. Write them down and examine their validity. Are these stories based on facts, or are they merely assumptions you've made over time?

Action:

List your answers: Write down the roadblocks you relate to, the areas where you feel stuck, and the stories you tell yourself. This will provide a clear starting point for action and help you recognize patterns that need to be addressed.

Exercise 2: Creating Your Breakthrough Plan

Now that you've identified the roadblocks and areas where you feel stuck, it's time to act. This exercise is about creating a tangible, actionable plan to break through your obstacles and start moving forward.

Questions to Reflect On:

1. **What is one small, tangible step you can take this week to move past your biggest roadblock?**
   Think about the roadblock that feels the most urgent or limiting in your life right now. What is one small, specific action you can take this week to begin breaking through that barrier? This could be as simple as scheduling time to work on a project, having a difficult conversation, or reaching out for support. Small actions create momentum, and taking one step forward will build confidence and clarity as you continue on your path.
2. **Who or what can support you in overcoming this challenge?**
   Identify who or what could help you overcome your roadblock. Is there a mentor, a friend, or a coach who can offer guidance or accountability? Maybe it's a resource, a book, or a program that can help you build the skills or mindset you need to overcome this obstacle. Determine who or what can provide the support and encouragement you need to stay on track and feel confident in your progress.
3. **What's the worst that could happen if you step fully into your power? And what's the best that could happen?**
   Often, fear holds us back from stepping fully into our power because we're afraid of the potential consequences. Reflect on the worst-case scenario. What are you really afraid of?

Now, contrast that with the best possible outcome. What could you achieve or experience if you stepped into your full potential? Visualizing both extremes can help you put your fear in perspective and motivate you to take action despite it.

Action:

Create your breakthrough plan: Write down the small step you'll take this week, the support you'll seek, and both the worst and best possible outcomes of stepping into your power. Commit to taking action, no matter how small, and revisit this plan regularly to measure your progress.

Ongoing Assessment:

Once you've completed these exercises, it's important to check in with yourself regularly to assess your progress. Revisit your answers, observe how you feel, and track your actions.

Ask yourself:

- Are the stories you told yourself still holding you back, or have you started to shift them?
- Has the action you've taken helped you make progress, even if it's just a small step forward?
- Who are your allies in this journey, and how can you lean on them for continued support?

By regularly assessing your progress, you ensure that you stay connected to your goals and accountable as you work through your roadblocks. Remember, taking action is not about achieving an unrealistic standard, but about creating forward momentum.

You Are Not the Problem—Your Roadblocks Are

If there's one powerful lesson to take away from this chapter, let it be this:

You are not the problem!

So often, we internalize our struggles, believing that something is inherently wrong with us when we encounter roadblocks. We think that if we haven't yet reached our goals or if things aren't moving as fast as we want them to, it's because of something flawed within ourselves. But that is simply not true. The problem isn't you—it's the roadblocks you're facing, the limiting beliefs, the fears, and the false narratives you've allowed to take up space in your mind.

Your doubts, fears, and limiting beliefs? They are not facts. They are patterns—patterns that have been built over time by experiences, societal conditioning, or past failures. These patterns are not permanent; they are just habitual ways of thinking that have become ingrained in your mind. But here's the thing about patterns: they can be broken. You have the power to disrupt these patterns and replace them with beliefs that serve you, that empower you, and that align with the woman you are becoming.

Think about this for a moment: **The version of you that is fully fulfilled, limitless, and thriving? She already exists.** She is within you, waiting to be set free. The thoughts, habits, and behaviors that have kept her hidden are the roadblocks. It's not about becoming someone new; it's about shedding the layers of self-doubt, fear, and negativity that have been placed on you over time. When you remove those blocks, you'll reveal the powerful, confident, and unstoppable woman who has always been there, ready to shine.

It's time to **clear the roadblocks**—to identify what's holding you back, challenge those limiting beliefs, and break free from the chains of fear and doubt. The process won't occur overnight, and there may be setbacks, but with each step forward, you are getting closer to your fullest self.

Let her through.

The woman who is capable of achieving her dreams. The woman who stands tall in her power. The woman who believes in her worth and has the courage to pursue the life she truly desires. She's not some future version of you—it's the woman you are right now, just waiting for you to remove the obstacles in your way.

This journey isn't about fixing yourself—it's about clearing the path for the fabulous woman you already are to step into the fullness of her potential. You are worthy. You are capable. And the only thing standing between you and the life you want is the roadblocks you've allowed to block your path.

So, let this be your reminder: **You are not the problem.** The roadblocks are. And you have everything you need to overcome them. It's time to start breaking the patterns and stepping into the life that is already waiting for you.

Remember you have access to a variety of assessments, journal exercises, and downloadables on the private book resources page here: www.LimitlessBookResources.com.

CHAPTER 11
Stop Settling And Ask For What You Need

The Life You Want Requires the Courage to Ask for It

"You are not hard to love. You are not too much. You are not asking for too much. Stop settling for people who make you feel otherwise."
– Alex Elle

Many of us, myself included, were taught from a young age to be nice, be quiet, smile, make others comfortable, shrink back, and don't inconvenience others with your needs or wants. Some of the messages are subliminal, and others are pretty obvious, but we don't want to inconvenience others. We want everyone to be happy. We inevitably become people pleasers and push down or minimize our needs over time.

I call bullshit on this idea! All this has really done is force us to hold ourselves back and not be our true selves. It also sends a message that we can't have what we want, we can't dream, or do anything that would make someone else feel bad, or outdo, or outearn someone else, or cause us to be the center of attention. But this also inevitably causes us to hide our gifts, which is the critical gap in our society today. We're so busy helping our children or spouses or friends become their best selves and doing things for other people that we don't believe that our gifts are meant to be shared with the world.

Even as a trailblazing woman constantly challenging the status quo at work and home, I can be very submissive in the name of being "supportive" and not wanting to disappoint those I love.

Here are some examples from my life that may resonate with you:

I once let my husband buy a house that I didn't want because he had already put in an offer against my wishes, and when the offer was accepted, I didn't want to disappoint him or the realtor who was about to make the sale or the seller who was about to sell their house. I went to the closing, and I signed the contract. I lived in a house that I absolutely hated for 10 years because I didn't want to make others uncomfortable or disappoint anyone. I lived with that decision every single day for 10 years, kicking myself. I tried to love the house. I upgraded everything. I moved things around and reorganized. I repainted and recarpeted. I changed out all the light fixtures. Over the course of 10 years, I literally replaced everything and finally completely redid the main level and....wait for it.... STILL hated it! Nothing worked. It wasn't the right house.

One simple example is that the master bedroom was designed in a way that the bed could only face one direction. I slept on the left side of the bed, so I had to sleep facing the door. I hated it! This meant that I was the first line of defense if either one of our kids came in during the night (or a burglar). Never mind that my husband can fall back asleep in minutes, and if I'm woken up, I'll lay awake for hours! I barely slept in that house. I wanted to feel safe and secure, and instead, I had to be on guard each and every night. For years, I was angry with my husband for buying a house I didn't want. Over time, I had to accept that it was just as much my fault as his and that I was stuck somewhere I didn't want to be. If I had simply had the courage to say NO and risk disappointing people, we would have found a different house that we both loved and not wasted all that money redoing everything in one I didn't want.

We finally got out of that house just a year ago when we built our dream house. You better believe I made sure that the bedroom had the flexibility to allow me to sleep away from the door! And even more so now, when I go to hotels and resorts, and they give me a room facing the door, I go down to the front desk and kindly ask them to move me to a different room. Sounds high maintenance? No! Why should I be uncomfortable to make others comfortable? Why are my needs less important than someone else's?

Same question back to you... Why should you be uncomfortable to make others comfortable? Why are your needs less important than someone else's?

Stop settling and ask for what you need!

How good are you at asking for what you need? Or asking for what you want? Does it make you feel guilty or empowered? Where are you "making do" to please someone else?

Here are some simple practices to try:

1. The next time you're out at a restaurant, and the waiter brings you the wrong dish or forgets the ketchup, or you need salt or anything at all, actually flag down the waiter and ask to make it right. This is not an inconvenience! You are a paying customer, and you're paying for a positive experience. This is no trouble at all. This also goes for dietary needs. If you need something gluten-free, or you want them to hold the cheese or cook it in butter instead of hydrogenated oils... Ask away!

2. The next time you're at a hotel, and you need extra pillows or a toothbrush, or the room is dirty, call down to the front desk and ask for someone to bring what you need to the room. Or ask to switch rooms if it doesn't meet your expectations. There's no point being uncomfortable all night long when you could restfully sleep.

3. Think about other ways you could use support in your daily life or to achieve a big goal.

- Do you need someone to watch the kids so you can start writing your book or go to that workout class? Ask your spouse, partner, a friend, or a neighbor to watch them for you, or hire a babysitter.
- Are you struggling to plan your meals and get healthy food on the table? Try one of the hundreds of meal services that are now available to make things faster and easier. The services range from someone making a meal plan for you and providing a grocery list to having the food delivered in perfect quantities so you can make dinner quickly to everything being ready-made and you just heat and serve.

- Experiment until you find something that works for you and your family.
- How about booking a massage once a month to get away and relax and have someone take care of you for an hour?
- And my personal favorite… Hire a house cleaner! Are you struggling to keep up with the never-ending cycle of laundry, dishes, or vacuuming? Try hiring a house cleaner, even if it's only once a month to start. This one is a total game-changer! Plenty of services offer this, so feel free to get multiple quotes to find someone who meets your expectations and budget.

This was the first splurge I did for myself 10 years ago, and it's the last thing I will ever give up. I absolutely hate cleaning and cannot keep up with my busy schedule. Twice every other week, I come home, and the angels sing when I walk in the door because the house is spotless! Try it on yourself; it will change your life.

Over time, asking for what you need builds your confidence and helps you see how valuable you are and what you bring to the world. It also makes you open to new ideas that you previously might have thought were an inconvenience to someone else.

God has given you extraordinary gifts that you likely don't see as extraordinary since they come so easily to you to do it. They can't! YOU can because that's what makes you special and important. Those are the gifts that you are to share with the world. And rather than thinking, "Who am I to do the thing?" I'd like you to shift your perspective to, "How am I doing a disservice to others by not sharing these gifts? How will I reach my full potential and the ultimate purpose that I was put on this earth to do if I don't share my gifts?" We need you!

Start changing your perspective by asking for what you need. Then, see how it starts to change your mindset and everything else. Before you know it, you'll be crushing your goals because you'll have the confidence and support you need to keep moving forward daily.

CHAPTER 12
Celebrate Your Wins & Savor The Joys In Life

Give Yourself Credit. You've Come So Far.

"If you only celebrate when you've hit the big goal, you'll miss 99% of your life. Celebrate progress, not perfection"
– Mel Robbins

I want to start with a full admission: I am not naturally good at celebrating or savoring accomplishments. Learn from me. I feel like I'm wired to check a box, move forward, and immediately ask, What's next? That tendency has served me well in my career and personal growth, but it has also robbed me of the joy of truly appreciating what I've achieved.

There have been times when I've looked at my life—objectively, a great life—and felt disconnected from joy. I couldn't quite figure out why. I should have felt more fulfilled. But when I reflected on it, I realized part of the issue was that I wasn't allowing myself to celebrate my successes. Instead of acknowledging how far I had come, I was always laser-focused on what still needed to be done.

I know I'm not alone in this.

Many high achievers struggle with celebrating their wins. Entrepreneurs, executives, and goal-driven individuals tend to focus on "the gap" instead of "the gain."

Are You Living in the Gap?

In the book *The Gap and The Gain*, authors Dan Sullivan and Dr. Benjamin Hardy describe how successful people often measure themselves against their ideal rather than their progress. The "gap" is that space between where you are and where you think you should be. No matter how much you accomplish, there's always more to do. The to-do list never ends, and the next big goal is always on the horizon.

When you live in the gap, you're constantly focused on what's missing. You tell yourself things like:

- Yes, I did X, Y, and Z, but I still haven't accomplished A, B, and C.
- I hit my revenue goal, but I haven't scaled the way I wanted.

- I launched the business, but it's not as big as I imagined it would be by now.

Living this way means you never quite feel satisfied. You don't let yourself enjoy the success you've already achieved because you're too focused on what's next.

The alternative is living in "the gain." This means measuring yourself against where you started. Instead of focusing on what's missing, you recognize your progress.

- Last year, I didn't even have a business. Now I have paying clients!
- A year ago, I had no idea how to invest in real estate, and now I own my first rental property.
- Six months ago, I struggled to work out consistently, and now I've hit 77 workouts!

It's such a small shift in perspective, but it changes everything. Instead of feeling frustrated that you're not "there" yet, you feel proud of how far you've come. And when you feel proud and accomplished, you're more motivated to keep going.

The Moment I Realized I Needed to Celebrate More

I remember a conversation with one of my mentors where I was venting. I dumped all my stress on her, telling her how overwhelmed I felt, how there was too much going on, and how I wasn't sure why I was doing all of it.

She stopped me mid-sentence.

She said, "Do you hear yourself? You're listing everything you haven't done, but all I can see is someone wildly successful. Have you even looked at what you've accomplished?" I was taken aback. She challenged me to write down everything I had achieved in the last year. And not just the "big" things—everything. The small wins. The incremental progress. The moments of growth. **It was a game-changer.** I realized I had done so much. But because I wasn't acknowledging it, it felt like nothing. That conversation taught me the power of pausing to reflect on wins—not just once a year, but regularly.

The Power of Writing It Down

Since that moment, I've made it a habit to track my wins. I actually have a page in my planner dedicated to this. Writing things down helps me see my progress in a way that's impossible to ignore. Even when it feels like I'm not doing enough, I can look at my list and say, "Wow. I've accomplished so much already."

Here are a few things I wrote down from a recent year:

- Increased my strength training workouts from 45 to 77.
- Grew The Powerhouse Women Network from eight women to over 77 in less than one year. What made this even more incredible was it happened organically based on referrals and private invites. True connection is something powerhouse women need and crave. We need a safe space to be free and not have to be "on" all the time.
- Traveled to Cancun, Florida, Italy, Greece, Georgia, and Seattle.
- Completed various home maintenance projects, including painting the deck, repainting walls, and sealing the front porch.
- Helped my youngest son start soccer and basketball.
- Finally, potty-trained my son Mason (this felt like my biggest win of the year!).
- Invested in my personal growth through coaching, inner healing, and Sozo sessions.

- Created new content for my business.

These big and small accomplishments added immense value to my daily life. I wasn't giving myself credit. I was in the gap.

How about you? Where are you living in the gap?

Exercise: Write down everything you have achieved in the past year.

Go through your calendar, photos on your phone, and your bank account or credit card statement to help you remember everything you did or invested in.

Write it all down, and spend time reflecting on how far you've come. Celebrate!

Ways to Celebrate and Savor

Acknowledging your wins is essential. But celebrating them is just as crucial.

So how do we do this?

1. Create Rituals of Celebration

Instead of letting big milestones pass unnoticed, build a habit of celebrating. That could mean:

- Toasting yourself with champagne.
- Taking a day off to relax and savor the moment.
- Going to dinner with a friend or your spouse to celebrate.
- Booking a spa day or getting a massage.

I personally love celebrating with experiences—whether it's a vacation with my husband or a luxurious meal with great food and wine.

2. Find Small Joys Daily

Celebration doesn't have to be reserved for major milestones. You can savor the little things, too.

- Savor your morning coffee instead of rushing through it.
- Take time to appreciate a great workout.

- Enjoy a sunset or a slow walk outside.
- Give yourself a high five in the mirror. (Thank you, Mel Robbins!)
- Pump your fist in the air and yell "Yes!" to release feel-good hormones like dopamine and endorphins.

The more you train yourself to recognize small joys, the easier it becomes to appreciate the big ones.

3. Regular Check-Ins

Ask yourself:

- How do I feel right now?
- What's going well?
- What needs work?
- What will I do differently?

I use my planner to write down what I have accomplished each week. Even a simple sentence about what I did yesterday helps me track my progress. These mini reflections keep you grounded in gratitude.

4. Give Yourself Permission to Rest

Many high achievers struggle to take breaks. I know I do. But rest is necessary.

Take at least one day off per week. Take a personal retreat for two to three nights minimum once per year. Get away for a kid-free vacation with your partner. Take time at the end of each year to truly rest and refocus. Rather than getting caught up in the chaos of holiday gatherings, spend time resting, giving yourself credit for your hard work, and refocusing on what's next for you. I have implemented all of the above practices, and each is a gentle reminder that constantly pushing isn't sustainable. Rest is a form of celebration, too.

5. Use Accountability & Support

Some people thrive with external accountability. If that's you, hire a coach, join a mastermind, or find an accountability partner. A good mentor or coach will remind you to celebrate what you've done—not just push toward the next thing.

Action Steps: Implementing Celebration & Savoring

1. Make a List of Your Wins

- Set a timer for 10 minutes, and write down everything you've accomplished in the last year.
- Include personal, professional, and growth wins.
- Don't minimize small accomplishments—they add up!

2. Plan a Celebration

- Pick one recent achievement, and plan a way to celebrate it.
- Book a massage, plan a special dinner, or take the day off.

3. Build a Habit of Gratitude

- Every morning, write down three things you accomplished the day before.
- At night, reflect on what you're grateful for.

4. Share Your Wins

- Tell a friend, mentor, or spouse what you're proud of.
- Celebrate with someone. Joy multiplies when shared.

The truth is, you are *already* successful. You don't have to wait to celebrate. Life is happening now. Savor it. Enjoy it! And permit yourself to feel the joy of recognizing just how much you've already accomplished.

Fulfilled & Limitless

One last thought that I want to leave you with as I close out this chapter on celebrating and savoring your wins is that sometimes what you celebrate and savor doesn't have to be an accomplishment. Sometimes it's learning a key lesson or shifting your mindset.

I met up with a friend recently because I wanted to hear all about her experience climbing Mount Kilimanjaro in Africa. I know several others who have done it and was evaluating whether or not I should add it to my goals list. She had come back a few months ago, and I was excited to hear about her trip and what she had learned. After telling me what an incredible experience it was, how beautiful it was there, and how good it felt to accomplish it, she admitted that it wasn't as big of a deal as she had thought and that she was expecting to feel more excited about it than she did. She felt like it had become something that she just checked off her to-do list. I asked her what she had learned from it, and she wasn't sure yet. However, she did mention that she noticed that while she was climbing, she was constantly thinking ahead and asking her guide how much longer it would be before they got to camp, would tomorrow be more or less rocky than today, and did he think that she was capable of finishing? Eventually, her guide asked her to stop and take in all the beauty around her. Truly look around and notice the flowers that only grow on Mount Kilimanjaro and the beautiful scenery around her. He suggested she be present and enjoy the moment so the experience wouldn't pass her by. After she shared her story, we had a beautiful conversation about the importance of presence and that perhaps that *was* the lesson for her. Sometimes the seemingly simple realizations can be the most profound. And that is worth celebrating.

I shared with her that I had had a similar experience on my recent trip to Thailand. I had expected to go to Thailand and have a major epiphany on what I was to do next and have a major takeaway or learning from it, but instead, while I was there, I simply had a *really amazing* time with fantastic people, and I deeply enjoyed the experience! Perhaps I finally learned how to enjoy my life and how to be grateful for each moment. For example, our group woke up at 4:30 in the morning to climb up to the top of Pu Chi Fa in the dark. Put that on the list of top 10 things I would *never* do on my own and never even have the desire to do, but I did it because our guide recommended it, and I'd signed up for the trip, so I wasn't going to miss out on what everyone else was doing. It turned out to be one of the most impactful things I did on that trip. It was the most *spectacular* view! It was such a fabulous experience, and all I could think about was how lucky I was to be at the top of that mountain, looking at the beautiful scenery around me and how thankful that I've been able to build a life where I get to do incredible things and have incredible experiences like this! That was a really profound realization for me because I simply soaked in the gratitude and the joy of the moment and the beauty all around me. I had a similar experience when we were at an elephant sanctuary in Thailand. We were doing yoga together as a group, and several elephants slowly walked by us. Again I had the realization that this is my life! I get to do yoga surrounded by elephants! That I've built a life where I can take amazing trips with amazing people and have incredible experiences while enjoying delicious food. What an absolute gift! I really was savoring each moment.

Five years ago, I definitely wouldn't have been able to say the same thing. I was always thinking about where I was going next and how I would get there. Every time I accomplished something, I would check it off my list and look forward to the next thing, the next, and then the next. I had a really hard time celebrating anything. If someone told me good job or congratulations, I would shake it off and say, "Oh, that's no big deal." I would think, "You should see what I'm going to do next." I didn't realize how sad that was then, but I definitely didn't feel fulfilled. I felt like there was always one more thing to do, one more ladder to climb, and one more achievement to accomplish. Over time, the more I did and achieved, the more I realized that it never felt like enough and that the feeling I thought I would have once I achieved my goal never actually materialized. I didn't enjoy it. I didn't celebrate. I didn't savor it. The title, the money, the accolades, and the awards just didn't mean what I thought they would mean to me once I got there.

Eventually, I had to acknowledge that just achieving one more thing wouldn't help me reach my ultimate goal of fulfillment. Instead, I had to look inward and think about what it would take to enjoy my life daily. What did I want my days to look like? The mundane and small moments of daily life? At the time, I didn't even know what I really liked. I had to start by creating a note on my phone, and every time I noticed something I liked, I had to write it down. It took me several months, but I've written down things like the smell of freshly cut grass, beautiful flowers, freshly cut flowers in my house for me to look at, beautiful fields filled with flowers, and the ocean breeze on my face. The taste of delicious, full-fat ice cream, or the taste of a full-bodied, red wine. The peaceful, serene sound of ocean waves. The feel of fuzzy blankets against my skin. Hearing the sound of my son laughing, seeing my kids learning a new skill, or seeing the joy on their faces while they laughed their heads off at a silly joke. Those are the things that brought me joy. Those were the things to celebrate and savor. How could I build more of those into my life?

Around the same time, I also started a gratitude practice, but rather than writing down all the big things I'm thankful for like my husband, our home, our jobs, our kids, our health... all things that I, of course, am extremely grateful for; I instead focused on the small things. Like the cozy feeling of a warm cup of tea in my hands or being able to sit in silence and enjoy the peace and quiet. Like the morning sunrise or how much I enjoy journaling and writing, sitting in front of the fire at night cuddling with my husband, watching a movie, and having lunch with a friend I hadn't seen in a while.

Those two practices of determining what I genuinely enjoy and starting a gratitude practice helped me shift my focus to seeing all the blessings in my life and savoring the small joys each day. My focus and my mindset completely changed! Rather than being a negative, anxious person, I became positive, happy. I saw the good in people. I saw the beauty around me. I enjoyed the present moment that I was in, rather than thinking ahead to the future I was trying to create or thinking about past regrets. Staying grounded in the present truly drives fulfillment.

I hope that you, too, will start these practices. Pay attention to what brings you joy, and start noticing those things all around you. I promise your whole life will change, and true fulfillment will become a normal way of life.

Exercise:

Make your own list of what brings you joy. Don't stop until you have at least 50 things on your list.

Action: start a daily gratitude practice. Write down three to five small things you notice each day and are thankful for.

CHAPTER 13
Keeping The Momentum
Your Fulfillment Audit & Roadmap

"You are truly amazing. Never give up or back down. Keep going!"
– Christi Cossette

Fulfillment isn't something you achieve once and then set on autopilot. It requires ongoing reflection, realignment, and intentionality. You've done the deep work in this book—unpacking your identity, redefining what fulfillment means, setting boundaries, and taking ownership of your energy, relationships, and impact. Now, the real challenge begins: **sustaining it**.

This chapter is best utilized at the end of each year in November or December. It will help you assess where you are now, celebrate your wins, identify what needs to shift, and create a **fulfillment roadmap** for the next year. The goal is to make sure you are **continuously refining and expanding**, rather than slipping back into old patterns.

Step 1: Reflect on Your Past Year—The Fulfillment Audit

Before you can create a powerful plan for the future, you need to assess where you've been. **Answer the following questions honestly.**

Energy & Well-Being

1. Over the past year, did your daily routines support your energy and well-being? If not, what needs to change?
2. What were your biggest energy drains? (List the top three.)
3. What activities, people, or habits gave you energy and made you feel most alive?
4. If you could change one thing about how you protected and managed your energy this year, what would it be?

Time & Priorities

1. Looking at how you spent your time this year, did your schedule align with your values? If not, what needs to change?
2. What were the top three things that consumed most of your time? Were they aligned with what truly matters?
3. What commitments, obligations, or distractions did you say "yes" to that you wish you had declined?
4. What was the most meaningful use of your time this past year?
5. What is one way you will be more intentional with your time next year?

Money & Resources

1. Over the past year, did you use money in a way that supported your values? (Y/N)
2. What were your best financial decisions this year?
3. What were your most significant money leaks or unnecessary expenses?
4. What is one change you will make next year to ensure your finances align with your priorities?

Relationships & Support System

1. Were your closest relationships supportive of your growth and fulfillment this year? (Y/N)
2. Who were the most energizing and inspiring people in your life this year?
3. Were there relationships that drained you or no longer aligned with who you are becoming? (List them privately.)
4. What boundaries do you need to set to protect your emotional and mental energy next year?

Work, Purpose & Impact

1. Did your work feel meaningful and aligned with your values? (Y/N)
2. What part of your work gave you the most fulfillment this year?
3. What part of your work felt draining, misaligned, or unsustainable?
4. If you could shift one thing about how you approach your career, business, or impact next year, what would it be?

Step 2: Define Your Next Year—Your Fulfillment Roadmap

Now that you've assessed what worked and what didn't, let's set a **clear plan** to move forward **with intention.**

1. Recommit to Your Core Values

From the values work you did earlier in this book, revisit your **top five values,** and make sure they are reflected in your next year.

Core Value	One Way You Will Prioritize This Value Next Year
1. _____	_____
2. _____	_____
3. _____	_____
4. _____	_____
5. _____	_____

Challenge: Where have you drifted from your values?

What **needs to change** for you to live in full alignment?

2. Identify Your Three Big Priorities for the Year

Instead of setting a laundry list of goals, focus on **three key areas** that will make the biggest difference in your fulfillment.

Focus Area	Why This Matters	First Step to Take
1. _____	_____	_____
2. _____	_____	_____
3. _____	_____	_____

Challenge: How will you hold yourself accountable for these priorities? Who or what will help you stay on track?

3. Create Your "Let Go" List

True transformation doesn't just come from **adding** new habits, priorities, or goals—it comes from **letting go** of what no longer serves you.

What are three things you will stop doing next year to protect your energy, values, and fulfillment?

1.

2.

3.

Final Step: Your Fulfillment Commitment

You've done the work. You've assessed your energy, time, money, relationships, and impact. Now, it's time to **commit to living in full alignment.**

Write a personal declaration to yourself. What kind of year are you going to create? How will you show up differently?

My Personal Example:

My mission is to inspire others to reach their full potential! This is the legacy I hope to leave.

I am a game-changer, a leader, a force to be reckoned with. I am a wife, a mother, a friend, an encourager, and a connector. I am a positive influence, a fighter; I never give up! I am changing the world by helping others achieve their full potential, changing the status quo, forging new paths that didn't exist before, and funding ministries worldwide.

I am a trailblazer! A powerhouse!

My purpose is to model the way forward. To help fellow powerhouse trailblazers to refresh and regain the courage to keep going. I create space to pause, reflect, celebrate, restore strength, encourage, and then refocus on goals and dreams to develop a plan of attack.

I want to be known as someone who stood up for those who couldn't stand up for themselves. Who brought darkness into the light. Who empowered others to step into their calling. Who helped people grow and reach their full potential. Who protects, guides, loves, leads, grows, and impacts. I want to be known as someone who inspires others. Who leads by example. Who builds people up. Who loves people and stands up when necessary. I want to drive good decisions and be known as someone who gets stuff done. Above all, I want to be a fantastic wife and mother. I want to raise healthy, godly, honorable, strong, courageous men of God who lead our world with integrity and love.

I don't know about you, but every time I read this out loud to myself, it makes me want to stand like Amy Purdy in the Superwoman pose. It makes me feel like I can do anything.

Christi Cossette

What about you? The sky is the limit! Who are you becoming? What is your legacy? How will you lead with purpose and impact your family, your community, and our world?

You already have everything you need! Go get it!

Now, write yours:

You've just made a powerful declaration about the kind of life you're committed to creating. That statement is your compass—a reminder of who you are and what matters most. But intention alone isn't enough. To truly anchor your vision into your daily life, you must reinforce it consistently. That's where the power of spoken words comes in.

Speak Life Over Yourself

> *"Death and life are in the power of the tongue. Words kill, words give life; they're either poison or fruit—you choose"* Proverbs 18:21 (The Message)

Your voice has authority. One of the most powerful ways to reinforce your identity, purpose, and vision is by speaking truth over yourself—**out loud**, every day. When you speak truth over yourself, you shift your mindset, elevate your energy, and train your brain to focus on what aligns with your highest self. Affirmations are not just motivational—they're transformational. They are declarations that rewire your brain, shape your self-concept, and anchor you in the life you're building.

Start or end your day with affirmations that align with your goals and values. You don't need dozens—just a few powerful, personalized statements that remind you who you are and what you're here to do.

This final step is about making your commitment *stick* by embedding it into your everyday routine. Let your words shape your world. Speak life over yourself, and watch your fulfillment become your reality.

Exercise: Identify Five to Ten Daily Affirmations to Support your Vision and Goals

Some examples to get you started:

- I lead with courage, compassion, and conviction—creating space for others to rise with me.
- I no longer shrink to fit into places I've outgrown—I walk boldly in rooms I once only dreamed of.
- I am building a life that reflects my values, not just my obligations.
- I release the need to prove my worth—I am already more than enough.
- I create healthy boundaries that protect my peace and preserve my power.
- I honor my body as the sacred vessel of my calling—rested, nourished, and strong.
- I am fully present with my children, knowing they don't need perfection, just my love and presence.
- I don't chase validation—I attract aligned opportunities by being my authentic self.
- I welcome wealth, wisdom, and divine guidance—I am open to receiving all that is meant for me.
- I walk in purpose, knowing that my work is meaningful and my impact is lasting.
- I no longer carry guilt for having ambition—my dreams are an extension of God's design in me.
- I allow joy and fun into my life without guilt—play is part of my power.
- I forgive myself for past decisions and choose to move forward with grace and clarity.

- I choose to trust the timing of my life—I am exactly where I need to be.
- I am a cycle-breaker, a legacy-builder, and a voice for what's possible.
- I give myself permission to change, evolve, and become someone new.
- I show up in rooms as the woman I'm becoming—not the one I've been.
- I protect my time like a sacred resource—my calendar reflects my priorities.
- I nurture relationships that energize, elevate, and expand me.

Write your own. Speak them out loud daily. Your words shape your world.

Your Future Is Built One Decision at a Time

Everything you've learned in this book leads to this: **The life you want is created by the decisions you make every day.** No one is coming to give you permission. No one is going to build your fulfilled and limitless life for you.

But you can.

You already know what needs to change. You already have the roadmap. Now, it's time to live it!

Are you ready? Then let's go.

CONCLUSION:
A Love Letter To You

Own Your Story.
Live Your Purpose.
Walk in Power.

"Own your story, stop settling, and rise to all God created you to be—bold, whole, and wildly fulfilled. The world needs your gifts. Don't hold back."

—Christi Cossette

Let's go back to where we started. Remember the values assessment and life alignment check-in? The moment you took an honest look at where you are today and where you long to be? That was the first step—awareness. Now, after walking through this journey together, you have the tools, the framework, and the vision to step into your fulfilled and limitless life.

So, what's next for you?

Do you need to set a bold new goal? Hire a coach? Schedule a long-overdue vacation? Set boundaries in a relationship that's been draining you? Make the move you've been hesitating on? Whatever it is, I encourage you—no, I **urge** you—to take the first step. Because the world needs you.

Your gifts.

Your wisdom.

Your leadership.

Your heart.

Your voice.

If there's one thing I hope you take away from this book, it's this: You were not created to live a small life. You were meant for more. You were designed to be strong, to create, to expand, to love deeply, and to step boldly into the purpose God has placed within you.

I know what it's like to feel stuck, to carry the weight of expectations, to put yourself last, to wonder if it's too late, too hard, too selfish, too much. But I also know what it's like to break free. And that's what I want for you.

No more waiting. No more shrinking. No more holding yourself back.

Fulfilled & Limitless

I am fulfilled—not because life is perfect (it never will be), but because I am walking in alignment with my purpose. I am deeply loved, and I love deeply in return. I have faith in God's plan. I take care of my body, nurture my mind, and surround myself with people who uplift and challenge me. I live with joy, knowing that fulfillment isn't a destination—it's a way of being. And every day, I wake up choosing it.

And you can, too.

So, what is fulfillment, really? How will you know when you're there?

Fulfillment isn't just about success, wealth, or achieving goals (though those are all beautiful byproducts of purpose-driven living). Fulfillment is peace. It's waking up excited about your life. It's knowing you're living with intention. It's surrounding yourself with people who genuinely love, admire, and respect you. It's putting God first, family second, and building a life and career that align with your values. It's about giving, growing, multiplying—because when we are faithful with what we've been given, more is always added.

There will be seasons where your dreams take a backseat—when you're caring for a sick child, navigating loss, or healing your own body and mind. That's okay. Life isn't a straight path, and fulfillment isn't about doing everything at once. It's about knowing when to push forward and when to pause. It's about trusting the process, trusting yourself, and trusting God.

And when you get knocked down? When you fail? When it feels like everything is working against you?

You keep going.

You get up again and again.

You step forward in faith, even when you can't see the whole path.

You refuse to settle.

Because this is your one life. And I want you to live it fully.

I am cheering for you. I believe in you! And I know that whatever is in your heart—the vision you see, the dream you feel—it's there for a reason.

So take the next step.

Break the barriers.

Become everything you were created to be.

Never settle.

I want you to know that I'm praying for you. I'm praying for you to come out of your box, whichever boxes others have put you in or that you have chosen to stay in due to any limiting beliefs you've developed throughout your life. I'm praying for your freedom and that you will step into your calling and all that you were created to be.

With love, blessings, and unshakable belief in your limitless potential,

Christi

About The Author

Christi Cossette is a sought-after executive coach, transformational speaker, and International Best-Selling author dedicated to empowering high-achieving women to reconnect with their purpose and redefine success on their own terms. As the founder of **Cossette Transformation Coaching**, she helps ambitious women navigate career transitions, elevate their leadership, and create more fulfilling lives through strategic executive coaching and transformative frameworks. Drawing on over two decades of experience in business transformation and leadership, Christi has guided powerhouse women through pivotal career shifts, entrepreneurial ventures, and life-changing breakthroughs.

Christi is also the founder of **The Powerhouse Women Network**. In this private community, ambitious women cultivate deep connections while navigating executive leadership challenges. Designed for six-figure entrepreneurs and senior executives, members gain access to expert insights, authentic support, and high-impact relationships with women who understand their ambitions and challenges.

Christi's mission is to inspire women to reach their full potential without losing themselves in the process. In *Fulfilled & Limitless*, Christi blends personal stories, actionable strategies, and her signature **Fulfilled Life Formula** to inspire women to design lives of impact, freedom, and lasting fulfillment. She lives in Minnesota with her husband, Andy, and their three sons.

Learn more about Christi at ChristiCossette.com

Bibliography

Bethel Church, *Sozo Inner Healing Ministry*. Redding, CA: Bethel Church. www.Bethel.com/ministries/sozo-international

Blakely, Sara. Referenced as the founder of Spanx and an example of entrepreneurial resilience. See: *Forbes* profiles and "How I Built This" interview.

Breathwork healing modalities referenced from various somatic and nervous system regulation techniques. See also: www.BreathWork.com/

Clear, James. *Atomic Habits: An Easy & Proven Way to Build Good Habits & Break Bad Ones*. New York: Avery, 2018.

Duffield-Thomas, Denise. *Money Bootcamp*. www.Denisedt.com/bootcamp

Dare to Believe. *Dare to Believe Ministries*. Burnsville, MN. dtbmn.org

Dweck, Dr. Carol S. *Mindset: The New Psychology of Success*. New York: Ballantine Books, 2006.

Estima, Stephanie. *The Betty Body: A Geeky Goddess' Guide to Intuitive Eating, Balanced Hormones, and Transformative Sex*. Hay House, 2021.

Hardy, Benjamin, and Dan Sullivan. *The Gap and the Gain: The High Achievers Guide to Happiness, Confidence, and Success*. Hay House Business, 2021.

Jack's Basket. A nonprofit celebrating babies with Down syndrome. www.jacksbasket.org/

Johnson, Brian. *Heroic*. Philosopher and founder of Heroic Public Benefit Corporation. www.heroic.us/

Levine, Dr. Peter A. *Somatic Experiencing®*. Trauma Healing. traumahealing.org/

Purdy, Amy. *On My Own Two Feet: From Losing My Legs to Learning the Dance of Life*. New York: HarperOne, 2014.

Robbins, Mel. *The High 5 Habit: Take Control of Your Life with One Simple Habit*. New York: Hay House, 2021.

Roberts, Nancy Lynn. *Progress Not Perfection: A Meaningful Journey with Lasting Joy*. CreateSpace Independent Publishing Platform, 2012.

Rowell, Kristin. *Lean & Fit for Life*. Online course with lifetime access. Energetically Efficient, www.EnergeticallyEfficient.com. Accessed November 2023.

Sims, Stacy T., and Selene Yeager. *ROAR: How to Match Your Food and Fitness to Your Unique Female Physiology for Optimum Performance, Great Health, and a Strong, Lean Body for Life*. Rodale Books, 2016.

Van der Kolk, Bessel. *The Body Keeps the Score: Brain, Mind, and Body in the Healing of Trauma*. New York: Penguin Books, 2015.

Williamson, M. (1992). *A Return to Love: Reflections on the Principles of A Course in Miracles*. New York, NY: HarperCollins.

Winfrey, Oprah. *What I Know for Sure*. New York: Flatiron Books, 2014.

Additional Resources

The Fulfilled & Limitless Workbook

To compliment your experience, you can download printable versions of the exercises along with a workbook, bonus tools, and resources here: www.LimitlessBookResources.com.

The Fulfilled & Limitless Newsletter

I invite you to subscribe to my Fulfilled & Limitless Newsletter to further support your journey toward a fulfilled and limitless life. By joining, you'll receive exclusive content, practical strategies, and the latest updates on upcoming retreats and events designed to empower executive women like you. Subscribe at ChristiCossette.com/

The Fulfilled & Limitless Blog

Explore a wealth of insights and inspiration by visiting my blog, where I share articles on leadership, personal growth, and achieving alignment in all areas of life.

Read past blog posts here: ChristiCossette.com/blog/

Stay connected and continue your journey toward unparalleled success and fulfillment.

Fulfilled & Limitless Coaching

You've done the work. Now, it's time to go deeper.

You've read Fulfilled & Limitless.

You've reconnected with who you are, clarified your values, and maybe even started building a roadmap toward the life you truly want.

But some things can't be done alone.

The internal transformation is real—but now you're ready for strategic partnership and 1:1 support to bring it to life in bold, tangible ways.

This coaching isn't about repeating what you've already done.

It's about **refining, aligning, and accelerating** the vision you've started to build—so you can live it with more clarity, confidence, and impact than ever before.

This Is for You If...

- You've done the journaling, the exercises, the reflection—but something still feels stuck.
- You've started building a roadmap, but need guidance to *actually implement it* in your real life.
- You're craving personalized insight, strategic support, and honest feedback.
- You know where you're going—but need help navigating the messy middle.
- You're ready to break through old limits and lead from full alignment.

You don't need more theory. You need *targeted support* to help you apply what you've learned in a way that's tailored to you.

What We'll Do Together

In *Fulfilled & Limitless Coaching*, we'll take what you've already discovered and bring it to life with powerful, personalized support.

Whether you're navigating a leadership transition, setting stronger boundaries, rewriting old patterns, or pursuing a new vision—you'll have a trusted, strategic partner walking alongside you.

You'll get support in:

- Clarifying your next steps with confidence and focus
- Identifying and clearing lingering mindset or emotional blocks
- Refining your roadmap and aligning your life with your deepest values
- Making bold decisions from your empowered identity—not fear or pressure
- Staying grounded and accountable as you take brave action toward your fulfilled life

How We'll Work: The EMPOWERED Framework

Inside coaching, we use the **EMPOWERED Framework** as a flexible tool to deepen the work you've already begun. It serves as a lens to clarify where you're aligned—and where you're still stuck.

E – Embody Your Identity

M – Manage Your Energy

P – Practice Faith & Mindset Mastery

O – Own Your Life with Radical Responsibility

W – Work Through Your Wounds and Break Old Patterns

E – Elevate Your Relationships

R – Rediscover Purpose through Faith, Love, Service, and Meaningful Work

E – Embrace Celebration and Joy

D – Design a Life That Reflects It All

This isn't a curriculum—it's a process we customize based on your goals, challenges, and leadership season.

The Outcome?

✔ You'll stop spinning in indecision and start moving in alignment.

✔ You'll strengthen your voice, boundaries, and leadership presence.

✔ You'll create the space you need to flourish—personally and professionally.

✔ You'll experience what it means to be successful *and* fulfilled.

Let's Go Deeper Together

This is more than coaching.

It's a sacred container for powerful women who are done settling and ready to embody the fullness of who they are.

If you're ready for real transformation—with practical strategy, honest reflection, and deep soul support—this is your next step. Book a discovery call at ChristiCossette.com/Contact

You've already started the work.

Now let's finish what you came here to build.

The Powerhouse Women Network

Where High-Achieving Women Elevate Together

Success doesn't have to be lonely. You've built an incredible career or business, but where do you go to connect with women who truly get it—women who are just as ambitious, driven, and determined to create both impact and fulfillment?

Welcome to The Powerhouse Women Network—an exclusive community designed for high-achieving women executives and entrepreneurs who want to grow, scale, and thrive together.

This Is for You If...

- ☑ You're a successful executive, business owner, or entrepreneur generating $250K+ in revenue.
- ☑ You're looking for the right community—one that challenges, inspires, and supports you.
- ☑ You crave real conversations with powerhouse women who understand your level of success.
- ☑ You want high-value networking, expert-led masterclasses, and strategic connections to elevate your career or business.
- ☑ You're ready to step into your next level with a supportive, like-minded network.

What You Get Inside The Powerhouse Women Network:

Exclusive Events & Masterminds – Connect with powerhouse women through in-person and virtual events designed to fuel your growth

High-Value Networking & Referrals – Build meaningful relationships that lead to real opportunities and collaborations

Business & Leadership Development – Learn from top-tier experts, and gain insights to scale your business and career

A Trusted Inner Circle – Join a private, invite-only community of women who support, challenge, and celebrate each other's success.

Success Is Better Together—Join Us Today!

The Powerhouse Women Network isn't for everyone—it's for women who are playing at a high level and are ready to go even further with the right support.

If that sounds like you, we'd love to have you inside.

Apply Now to Join The Powerhouse Women Network at ChristiCossette.com/Powerhouse-Women-Network

Surround yourself with women who get you. Elevate your business. Expand your impact. Your next level starts here.

The Fulfilled & Limitless Executive Women's Retreat

You've spent your life achieving, leading, and making an impact—now it's time to invest in YOU.

Imagine stepping away from the daily grind to reconnect with your purpose, recharge your energy, and surround yourself with powerhouse women who truly understand your journey. The Fulfilled & Limitless Retreat is designed exclusively for high-achieving executive women and entrepreneurs who are ready to elevate their success while prioritizing their well-being.

What You Can Expect:

☑ Transformational Sessions – Elevate your mindset, redefine success, and break through limiting beliefs.

☑ Curated Connections – Connect with ambitious, like-minded women who inspire and challenge you.

☑ Luxury & Relaxation – Enjoy an immersive, high-end experience that blends personal growth with rejuvenation.

☑ Actionable Strategies – Leave with a clear vision and an execution plan to create more fulfillment in every area of your life.

This isn't just another retreat—it's an investment in the future you want to create. If you've been waiting for the right time to prioritize YOU, this is it.

Join Us for the Experience of a Lifetime

✦ Secure your spot now: ChristiCossette.com/retreat/

Seats are limited, and this retreat is by invitation or application only. Don't miss this opportunity to step into the next level of your life and leadership.

Your success isn't just about what you achieve—it's about how fulfilled you feel along the way.

Let's create that fulfillment together.

www.ingramcontent.com/pod-product-compliance
Lightning Source LLC
Chambersburg PA
CBHW050526100526
44581CB00008B/143/J